ENRIQUE GONZÁLEZ MARTÍNEZ

by

JOHN S. BRUSHWOOD

The literary production of Enrique González Martínez spans more than the first half of the present century. This study of the Mexican poet's work explains his search for ultimate, indestructible truth through the identification of himself with all created things. Even his earliest poetry expresses this need for reunion. Later, the poet's world becomes so complicated that he cannot capture the sense of being part of the whole; and for a while he is more observer than participant. With the death of his beloved, he again senses the reality of rejoining, through his awareness of her continued presence with him.

Dr. Brushwood specifically avoids deriving from the poetry any "message" that can be stated categorically in prose. Using non-technical language, he focuses on the creative act itself, inviting the reader to participate in this act with the poet. He examines the successes and failures of the poet's struggle, and emphasizes the magic moments when the poet's comprehension is expanded by the creative act until he sees, if only for a moment, a reality much more complete than the visible reality that men often take to be the whole truth.

TWAYNE'S WORLD AUTHORS SERIES

A Survey of the World's Literature

Sylvia E. Bowman, Indiana University

GENERAL EDITOR

MEXICO

John P. Dyson, Indiana University

EDITOR

Enrique González Martínez

(TWAS 88)

TWAYNE'S WORLD AUTHORS SERIES (TWAS)

The purpose of TWAS is to survey the major writers—novelists, dramatists, historians, poets, philosophers, and critics—of the nations of the world. Among the national literatures covered are those of Australia, Canada, China, Eastern Europe, France, Germany, Greece, India, Italy, Japan, Latin America, New Zealand, Poland, Russia, Scandinavia, Spain, and the African nations, as well as Hebrew, Yiddish, and Latin Classical literatures. This survey is complemented by Twayne's United States Authors Series and English Authors Series.

The intent of each volume in these series is to present a critical-analytical study of the works of the writer; to include biographical and historical material that may be necessary for understanding, appreciation, and critical appraisal of the writer; and to present all material in clear, concise English—but not to vitiate the scholarly content of the work by doing so.

Enrique González Martínez

By JOHN S. BRUSHWOOD

The University of Kansas

Twayne Publishers, Inc. :: New York

For Carolyn—
*"tú por quien la noche canta
y se ilumina el silencio"*

ABOUT THE AUTHOR

John S. Brushwood holds the Roy A. Roberts Professorship of Latin American Literature at The University of Kansas. He is a specialist in Mexican literature and has published extensively in this country and in Mexico. His most recent book is *Mexico in Its Novel: A Nation's Search for Identity* (Texas, 1966). Dr. Brushwood studied at Randolph-Macon College, the University of Virginia, and Columbia University. His literary investigations have made him a frequent visitor in Mexico. Before accepting his present appointment, Dr. Brushwood served as Professor of Spanish and Chairman of the Department of Romance Languages at the University of Missouri.

ENRIQUE GONZÁLEZ MARTÍNEZ

Preface

I suppose we are all surprised occasionally by how much we take for granted. In that moment when we stand apart from ourselves, in self-examination, we see how our reactions have been circumscribed by habit, or custom, or tradition, or inertia. In making this study of Enrique González Martínez, I have experienced a kind of reawakening of my response to his work, and have discovered how often I have made comments about it—perfectly valid, standard observations—without really feeling the poetic vibration.

Everyone agrees that EGM is one of the masters of twentieth-century Hispanic poetry. We admire him for his long and faithful —and often painful—poetic search. And we point out the particular beauty that emanates from the combination of man and poetry. Yet there has been astonishingly little penetrating study of his work. Titles are numerous, but depth is rare. And long studies are almost nonexistent. If it were not for the bibliographical work of Ana María Sánchez and the articles of José Topete, we would have practically no serious treatment of EGM since his death. Even Topete's articles appear to be based on a thesis, unfortunately not published, which was written during the poet's last years. He was in a position, however, to take into account virtually the whole trajectory of the poet's work. The serious studies written earlier are, of course, limited by time, though some of them are very perceptive. And we can also be grateful for a number of pieces written in praise of the poet—essays which are primarily eulogistic, but which do provide some valuable insights.

I rather think that we assume that more has been written about EGM than is actually the case. Whatever we assume, comments on his poetry have tended to follow certain lines that have by now become more or less standard. And repetition of the same selections in anthologies has paralleled this criticism. The poet's relationship with *modernismo* is a *sine qua non*. The poetic ascension is usually mentioned in one way or another, and we generally regard EGM's poetic journey as a straight road upward, without taking account of the difficulties or the hesitation.

Usually we find some reference to a vanguardist influence in his middle years, but we rarely find clarification of the influence. And frequently, there are allusions to EGM's political position in some of his later poetry, but its meaning is not indicated. All these comments are important, and in general they are valid. The trouble with them is that they tend to oversimplify a very complex body of poetry. Standardization of these observations tends to make us forget the subtleties of the poetry itself.

A less valid treatment of the poet is the attempt to incarcerate him in a single word, to show that he is a mystic, or a philosopher, or a pantheist. Such words do have a certain descriptive value, but at best they can only intimate an aspect of what the poet is.

I have tried not to define the poet, and I have been particularly careful not to derive a philosophy from his work. It is difficult to imagine a more ungracious misuse of poetry than the organization of a pattern of thought extracted from a poet's verses. I do not mean that we should ignore his rational process, but that we should absorb it as one part of the poetic communication. What I have tried to do in this study is allow the poetry to keep on being poetry, to open myself to EGM's poetic act, and to lay bare my reaction before the reader. The result I hope for is certainly not to produce a study that will take the place of reading the poetry, but to show my reader what an important experience EGM's poetry is. Perhaps my own reactions will make the experience even richer for someone else; perhaps some who will read only a part of his poetry may find, in what I have written, the necessary bridge from one piece to another.

There can be little doubt that a serious reader of this poetry will develop a deep respect for the author, just as I have done. In connection with this feeling, it is probably appropriate to say that my reference to the poet by use of his initials is in no sense disrespectful. I have chosen the initials because frequent use of the name González Martínez is awkward in English.

It will be apparent that EGM had a considerable gift for writing prose. However, he considered himself a poet, and that is the way we always think of him. Therefore, I have decided to mention his prose only where it might enhance the poetic communication. And since I have focussed the study this way, I have avoided reference to the technical aspects of the poetry except where such considerations seem to me to contribute sub-

Preface

stantially to appreciation of the poetic act. Even then, I have avoided, whenever possible, the use of terminology that strikes me as more erudite than descriptive.

The translations are mine. There are some reasonably good translations of EGM's poety, but not enough by any one translator to help very much, and not enough by all of them combined to satisfy the needs of this study. Since I should have had to do most of the translations in any case, I decided to do them all. My reader should understand that I have not even hoped to translate poetry into corresponding poetry. Without establishing a set of basic principles, I have tried to give an English version that retains the largest amount of what I find in EGM's work. I have sought not to change the sense of what he says; I have also sought—not always successfully, I fear—to avoid absurd English, since González Martínez does not write absurd Spanish. Translation of poetry is one of the most demanding tasks a writer can undertake. The only reasonable hope is that one may not betray the poet more than is absolutely necessary.

Grants made by the research committees of two universities, Missouri and Kansas, have afforded me both time and assistance. Thanks for many stimulating ideas and for scholarly cooperation go to Mary Shelley Hopper, who wrote a comprehensive examination on the poet, and to Carole Gilmore, my research assistant, whose sensitive reading acted as a stimulus to my own.

JOHN S. BRUSHWOOD
The University of Kansas

Note: A book by Topete was published after the present study was written. (*El mundo poético de Enrique González Martínez.* Guadalajara, Linotipografía "Fenix," 1967.) It does not add substantially to what the author had published earlier.

Acknowledgment

Ing. Héctor González Rojo has graciously authorized reprinting the portions of the works of his father, Enrique González Martínez, that are contained in this book.

Contents

Contents

Chronology

1871   April 13: Enrique, son of José María González and Feliciana Martínez de González, born in Guadalajara, Jalisco, Mexico.

1881   Began preparatory education after receiving primary training at home.

1885   EGM awarded prize for his translation of Milton's sonnet on his blindness.

1886   Began study of medicine. Poems in local periodicals.

1893   Received medical degree and began practice in Guadalajara. Wrote poems, stories, and criticism.

1895   EGM's father accepted directorship of school in Culiacán, State of Sinaloa. EGM accompanied parents and sister. Saw the sea for the first time. Began medical practice in Culiacán; six months later he moved to Sinaloa, capital city of the state.

1896   Met Luisa Rojo y Fonseca, his future wife.

1898   November 26: Married. Poetry published in Mexico City and in provinces.

1899   Birth of first son, the poet Enrique González Rojo.

1900   False report of EGM's death evoked expressions of regret from many men of letters. In response, EGM decided to publish a volume of poetry.

1901   Birth of daughter, María Luisa.

1903   *Preludios.* Birth of son, Héctor.

1904   Death of mother. Birth of son, Jorge, who died at the age of sixteen months.

1905   Went to Mexico City where he met many of the literary figures of the day: V. Salado Alvarez, J. Casasús, A. Nervo, J. Sierra, L. Urbina, J. Valenzuela. The residence of several months in Mexico City was not entirely satisfactory and he returned to Sinaloa.

1907   *Lirismos.* Published magazine, *Arte,* with Sixto Osuna.

1909   *Silénter.* Elected corresponding member of Mexican Academy.

1911 *Los senderos ocultos* (*The Hidden Paths*). Secretary General in Culiacán when Revolution broke out. Went to Mexico City. Became a *miembro de número* of the Mexican Academy. Joined the Ateneo de la Juventud (The Atheneum of Youth).

1912 Editorial writer for *El Imparcial*. Founded *Argos*.

1913 Undersecretary of Public Education and Fine Arts.

1914 Father died. Became Secretary General in Puebla.

1915 *La muerte del cisne* (*The Death of the Swan*). *Jardines de Francia* (*Gardens of France*), translations of French poets: Verlaine, Baudelaire, Heredia, Maeterlinck, Samain, Jammes, and others. Returned to Mexico City where he occupied several teaching posts.

1917 *El libro de la fuerza, de la bondad y del ensueño* (*The Book of Strength, Goodness, and Dream*). Edited the magazine *Pegaso*, with R. López Velarde and E. Rebolledo. Editorial writer for *El Heraldo de México*.

1918 *Parábolas y otros poemas* (*Parables and Other Poems*).

1920 Went to Chile as Minister Plenipotentiary. Met Pedro Prado and Gabriela Mistral.

1921 Minister Plenipotentiary to Argentina. Met L. Lugones, R. A. Arrieta, R. Rojas, A. Capdevila, H. Quiroga. Cultivated friendship with *Nosotros* group.

1923 *El romero alucinado* (*Bedazzled Pilgrim*).

1924 To Spain and Portugal as Minister Plenipotentiary.

1925 *Las señales furtivas* (*Subtle Tokens*). "Problemas mexicanos," address before the "Sociedad Económica Matritense de amigos del país."

1931 Returned to Mexico.

1933 Secretary General of the Administrative Council of the National Bank of Agricultural Credit.

1935 Death of wife. *Poemas truncos* (*Unfinished Poems*).

1937 *Auscencia y canto* (*Absence and Song*).

1938 *El diluvio de fuego* (*The Flood of Fire*).

1939 Death of his poet son, Enrique. *Rosas en el ánfora* (*Roses in the Amphora*).

1940 "Ultimo viaje" ("Last Journey"), poem on the death of Enrique González Rojo, published as dedicatory poem to third volume of Polis edition of EGM's collected verse.

1942 *Bajo el signo mortal* (*Under the Mortal Sign*).

1943 Founding member of "Colegio Nacional."

1944 *El hombre del buho (The Man Inspired by the Owl)*, first volume of autobiography. Awarded Manuel Avila Camacho literary prize.

1945 *Segundo despertar y otros poemas (Second Awakening and Other Poems)*.

1948 *Vilano al viento (Thistle in the Wind)*.

1949 *Babel*. Chairman of the organizational committee of the Congreso Continental Americano de Paz.

1951 *La apacible locura (Gentle Madness)*, second volume of autobiography.

1952 February 19: Died. *El nuevo Narciso y otros poemas (The New Narcissus and Other Poems)*.

CHAPTER 1

Toward the Authentic Voice

> For the first time it seemed to
> me that I heard my own voice
> in my verses—
> *The Man Inspired by the Owl*

I *The Literary Setting*

ELEGANCE and certainty, as they were understood in the framework of the late nineteenth century, describe the external mood of the literary world in those years. It was a time of gracious living, at least on the surface of reality: carriage rides through the park, ornate salons, melodramatic gowns, and flowers in the lapel. Of course, not everyone's life was so luxurious, but luxury was the ideal; and those for whom the ideal was beyond aspiration were generally forgotten. When they were remembered, it was with patient condescension or with the intention of exploitation—or perhaps a poetic soul might see in the humble a certain primitive goodness, or the reincarnation of a Neoclassical shepherd. Even if these attitudes suggest to the mid-twentieth-century mind a considerable degree of pretense, the large majority of Mexicans—and probably of most other Western peoples—were living, some seventy years ago, in the certainty that things were as they were simply because that was the way things were supposed to be. The literature of the time was equipped with a similar shining veneer. And underneath, literature shared with society a profound uneasiness, visible only to the eye that wished to see.

Enrique González Martínez was born less than four years after the execution of Emperor Maximilian, who had been imposed by the French and ultimately defeated by the Republic under Benito Juárez.[1] The fact of that elaborate and futile imperial design, viewed and somewhat romanticized in historical perspective, seems far removed from the lifetime of a twentieth-century poet, one who in fact was still writing less than two decades ago. We are deceived by the poetic vitality of EGM, who lived to be more than eighty years old and remained faithful to his poetic quest because he profoundly understood its timeless nature. It is hardly necessary to say that during those eighty years literary fashions came and went. EGM observed them, sometimes used them, at least once appeared to be overwhelmed by them; but through all of them he maintained the integrity of his search and self, and that is why his poetry seems neither old-fashioned nor particularly modern.

González Martínez grew up during the political regime of Porfirio Díaz, the more or less benevolent dictator who was the political power in Mexico for some thirty years prior to the Revolution that began in 1910. By the mid-1890's, EGM had finished his studies and had begun medical practice, and had also published poetry in provincial reviews and in Mexico City. By the same time, the Díaz government had acquired the aspect of an "establishment." Its insistence on political order, even at the expense of personal liberty, had produced a stable if stultifying effect throughout the whole society. The economy was sound and satisfactory from the standpoint of the middle class, and no one was prepared to take on the problem of the underdogs. There was a general feeling that Mexico had at long last become a modern nation. It would be only a slight exaggeration to say that Mexico's success was measured by the degree of similarity between Mexican customs and those of Europe, especially France. If there were underlying uncertainties, there was a general feeling of satisfaction on the surface.

The social condition had its parallel in literary expression. Perhaps some of the literary characteristics of the time were caused by the nature of the society, but in a more general sense, the literature grew with other constituents of the world of which it was a part. The most obvious problem was created by the presence of Realist and Naturalist influences in prose fiction. Realism had been a factor in prose fiction for quite a few years; its combination with Romanticism and its eventual acquisition of the dominant role had been gradual. The literary criticism of the time also makes it clear that the Mexicans had no particular interest in differentiating between Realism and Naturalism. Literary men argued about the merits of the new fiction and, in general, took the position that Realism-Naturalism did not see all of reality. They were concerned about the loss of certain spiritual values which can best be described as humanistic.

The real core of the problem lay deeper than this debate. The procedures of Realism and Naturalism, however they might be combined or separated, inevitably called for an honest view of the society. And if the novelists looked too carefully, what they saw might well be the instrument that would upset the stability that gave them the opportunity to write. Earlier generations of Mexican writers had been bedevilled by the chaotic state of the nation. It is perfectly understandable that the men who had been given the necessary conditions would hardly set about destroying them. There was indeed a problem of conscience, and the novelists, for the most part, took refuge in nineteenth-century attitudes that stressed individual improvement and took little account of the social obligation of the group. Many of the novels pictured social conditions that were far from ideal, but frantically sought values that would justify support of the status quo. This search for admirable qualities among the humble bears a certain similarity to the idealization of rustics that is found in a good deal of the poetry of the period.

Poetry flourished, inspired by the extraordinary combination of influences, motivations, techniques, and attitudes that are referred to as *modernismo* in Hispanic literatures. So numerous and disparate are the characteristics of this kind of poetry that a definition is practically impossible. Discussions about its origins, influences, characteristics, and effect have gone on for years, and they are as vibrant today as ever. There is no doubt that it was an American movement, insofar as it may safely be referred to as a "movement," and there is no doubt that it produced a very substantial body of excellent poetry. Its high priest was Rubén Darío, a Nicaraguan by birth who belonged, in a very real sense, to the whole Hispanic world. Darío was by no means the initiator of *modernismo*; he was rather the key, the name by which the phenomenon could be identified, the most typical and probably the best of its poets.

In Mexico, a combination of circumstances supported the founding of two of *modernismo's* most important reviews. The

Revista Azul was founded in 1894 and lasted until 1896; the more important *Revista Moderna* was published from 1898 until 1911. Practically every important literary name in Mexico was associated with one or both of these reviews, and it is equally important that the editors, particularly those of the *Revista Moderna,* were interested in making the magazines internationally representative rather than narrowly national. Their attitude illustrates what may well be the most basic characteristic of *modernismo,* its universality. Closely related to this attitude was a slightly more restricted one: the desire to be modern, to bring Mexican poetry up to date with the poetry of Europe. It is not hard to see the relationship between this attitude and Mexico's desire to be a modern nation, a desire which promoted the building of French-type houses in one of the capital's new and fashionable residential sections where the streets were named for European cities. Traditional Spanish influence remained, but the frivolous thought it was unsophisticated. The poets did not. The modern outlook afforded them a wonderful freedom from the tired poetic expression of the recent past; but looking farther back into the Hispanic tradition, they found both a discipline and an additional freedom in the work of Luis de Góngora and the other baroque poets.

The change from the recent past really meant growth outward from Romanticism toward a new expression. Romanticism had lost the fire that was the source of its poetic magic, and among the writers of the second generation, the phoenix was rare. Still, *modernismo* cannot rightly be considered a reaction against the Romantic outlook; in some ways it was a continuation: we find the same melancholy, the same love of the exotic, the same search for the ineffable. What was different was the *modernistas'* awareness of the creative act. Rather than try to capture the poetic concept in the familiar, tired phrase, they understood that the poetic moment depended on the word itself, on the ability of the word to contain the essence of poetry. The word and its use was a primary consideration, and this fact either reflects the influence of the French symbolists and parnassians or explains why the *modernistas* sought them out. From the French poets, they learned many techniques, particularly with regard to the adjective. Without going into a great many technical details, we may appreciate some of the effects by examining one of EGM's lines: "the silvery falling of your diaphanous drops" (*el caer argentino de tus diáfanas gotas*), from "Hidden Spring" ("Fuente oculta"), one of his earlier poems.[2] The word *caer* is the infinitive form of the verb that means "to fall." By using the definite article before it, the poet gives the word the same substantive value that "falling" has in English. He then chooses his adjective, "silvery." Note that "silvery" is not an adjective one would ordinarily expect to modify "falling." "Precipitous" or "violent" or a number of other adjectives would be more likely candidates. But by this unusual combination EGM gives his substantive a special value, and the nature of "falling" is completely controlled by the adjective. Because we know exactly what the poet is describing in this case, and because the image is immediately reinforced by "drops," the effect of the combination is not overly shocking. However, often the *modernista* poets used what we might call the "essential adjective" in places where the context is less cooperative.

A glance at the second noun-adjective combination shows that, unlike the first, it is a perfectly ordinary description. However, "silvery" could just as reasonably modify "drops" as "falling," and indeed, an interesting effect can be obtained by switching the two adjectives. While this particular usage could not be called a *modernista* technique, the poets frequently did gain effect by placing next to a noun an adjective which would modify the contiguous noun less commonly than it might modify another noun in the same phrase, e.g., the violent fear of the storm.

We may also notice a synesthetic effect in EGMs' line. The visual effect of "silvery" is associated with the aural effect of "falling" and "drops." Synesthesia, the association of two or more senses, was so common a technique among the *modernistas* that it could probably be called a characteristic. And in many cases, the use is far more surprising than it is here. The Uruguayan poet, Julio Herrera y Reissig, produced one of the all-time winners when he came up with "the gray sarcasm of her glove." Given the *modernista* love for color, it is natural that colors play a prominent role in synesthetic imagery. A fine example is EGM's "the cascade of your golden laugh" (*la cascada de tu risa de oro*) from "Laugh" ("Ríe"). (I.10) Here the aural value of "laugh" is combined with the visual of "gold," and both senses are incorporated into "cascade."

These examples of adjectival usages will furnish some idea of the complicated techniques of the poets who were writing when González Martínez was a young man. He used these techniques, indeed never entirely forsook them, but neither was he victimized by them. Of course, *modernista* techniques involved more than the ingenious use of adjectives. Poets found unusual combinations of noun and verb, produced unexpected personifications, experimented with repetition of sounds and the whole matter of rhythm in general. The doctrine of art-for-the-sake-of-art demanded beauty within the poem itself; and the whole effort was a striving toward the ineffable, an abstraction that was perfect beauty and was the source of inspiration and of melancholy at the same time.

There is no doubt that the insistence on beauty was also one of *modernismo's* functions within the literary world. It was a reaction against the ugliness of Realism-Naturalism. The two trends lived side by side and, of course, each had some influence on the other; however, it was the role of *modernismo* to supply some of the reality that Mexican men of letters thought was omitted by Realism-Naturalism. And the poets' search for beauty took them toward new themes as well as toward new techniques. The beauty they saw in material luxury sent their imaginations soaring toward marble palaces, their love of the exotic toward strange landscapes, a renewed interest in Classical literature toward gods and goddesses, satyrs, nymphs, and drawing-room shepherds. As important as any theme was eternal woman who appeared in many guises: Venus, champagne-sipping and silvery-voiced beauties of the salon, country lassies at once robust and seductive, even the enticingly simple middle-class working girl. Though it would be wrong to say that there is a consistent view of women throughout *modernista* poetry, it is probably fair to say that woman is expected to be both teasing and submissive, and that whatever the interpretation of the feminine constant, the poet uses woman as a means of discovering beauty or some aspect of beauty.

The *modernista* search served a very important purpose in the history of Mexican letters: it provided a kind of esthetic proving ground. The parnassian interest in perfection of form and of word gave the poets a degree of assurance they had never known under less disciplined influences. Symbolist suggestion carried them forward in search of the elusive, and sometimes illusory, goal that must be every poet's destiny. The individual products of the search, the poems each as a separate product of the artist's creativity, are widely varied, depending on the proportions of the many influences that may have been active in the creation of a particular piece. Some are statuesque, unemotional except for the total emotion evoked by the whole work. Others are beauty as revealed in the misty vagueness of a Renoir canvas, suggestive and haunting. Still others vacillate between immobile statue and Galatea. Some hold the poetic moment in such a way that reality is like a many-faceted jewel that turns in the light, and mocks the reader who would choose a single aspect. Many are admittedly superficial, brilliant toys; but the best, for all their surface glamour, pull the responsive reader into the artist's quest for durable, perfect beauty.

Literary historians have always been bothered by the problem of how to classify EGM. Certainly his early poetry falls within the scope of *modernismo,* but even those poems were often given the stamp of the author's personal and profound searching; and his later work, in which his personal search becomes more important, still bears the mark of the early influences. Faced with the question of whether or not to call EGM a *modernista,* Frank Dauster, in his history of Mexican poetry, changed the question slightly and gave a better answer than the original question could ever have evoked: "Instead of calling him the last *modernista,* we prefer to call him the purest of the symbolists." (*En vez de llamarlo el último modernista, preferimos llamarlo el más puro de los simbolistas.*)[3] The poet himself gave an adequate answer, though not a categorical one, in the discourse written on the occasion of his election as a *miembro de número* of the Mexican Academy.[4] He expressed a profound respect for the *modernistas* by finding no great poet in Mexico between Sor Juana Inés de la Cruz and Manuel Gutiérrez Nájera. He also explained the difference that he understood between the purely verbal and the spiritual content of *modernismo—* a statement that is very meaningful in connection with his poem "Wring the Swan's Neck" ("Tuércele el cuello al cisne"), (I. 150) from the volume *Los senderos ocultos* (*The Hidden Paths*). The poem was taken by many to be an anti-*modernista* manifesto; but in the light of EGM's statement it must be understood as a warning against the verbal pyrotechnics that sometimes were all that the poems contained. EGM defended the *modernista* poetry that sought depth. He had great respect for the creative act which is captured by "the taste for the virgin word."[5] He knew that his own search for the answers to questions raised by observant man was not fundamentally different from the *modernista's*, and he certainly believed in the miracle of poetry. An illustration of this position is his objection to his friend Amado Nervo's trying to establish a poetic doctrine in his later work.[6] From EGM's point of view, such an effort was contradictory to the nature of poetry. For him poetry did not illustrate a belief, but was in itself the creative act that discovers truth.

The specific material world of González Martínez was neither as glittering nor as "arty" as the world of *modernista* poetry, but it was a perfectly satisfactory one. His father was a school teacher, his mother an intelligent housewife who gently encouraged his literary interests.[7] His education was completed without incident, and he established his medical practice immediately after graduation. Interest in poetry came early and he gained his first recognition in poetry when, at the age of fourteen, he translated Milton's sonnet on his blindness. This poem, for those who do not recall it, is the one that ends with the line "They also serve who only stand and wait." We are not likely to find anything that could properly be considered influence of Milton in EGM's poetry, but it is entirely possible that the calmness of the English poet's own grappling with reality may have implanted itself in the spirit of the young Mexican. No one could be surprised by his interest in Poe, whose haunting rhythms appealed to almost all the poets of the era. EGM also translated a number of French poets, and later published—in 1915—a volume of these translations. Generally speaking, his choices are those that a *modernista* poet might be expected to make.

Within his own poetic world, González Martínez created satyrs and shepherds, goddesses of varying degrees of divinity, and landscapes that are sometimes real and sometimes artificial. He was certainly writing within the taste of his own time; but many of his pieces, even the early ones, reveal his own particular communication with nature, which was to become the basis of his poetic quest. He was working toward poetic maturity. But he was primarily a physician and there is every reason to believe that he intended to keep on being one. EGM's ultimate and complete transition into the literary world was not indicated by any circumstance of the early years. Although his work soon attracted the attention of other writers and critics, there was no reason at that time to think that he would become more than a Sunday poet.

II Preludios

In 1900, a literary friend wrote and published EGM's obituary in a Guadalajara paper, and the news spread throughout Mexican literary circles. Before the poet could put a stop to the rumors, several eulogies had appeared. Some friends had already urged González Martínez to publish a collection of his poems, but he was inclined to maintain his status as an amateur. The praise he was accorded on the occasion of his supposed death, however, gave him second thoughts. It was not that he was disposed to accept uncritically the rather emotional evaluations of friends on that occasion; rather, it was that he realized that if he had in fact departed this life, it was highly probable that one or another of his friends would have collected and published a volume of his poetry. So he set about going through his papers and arranging a selection. The result was *Preludios*, which was published in 1903.

The reader's first reaction to *Preludios* is that its author is a competent young poet, neither more nor less. EGM was already handling the tools of poetry with considerable skill. The volume contains a number of sonnets which show a sensitivity to the nuances of the language. The poetic mood varies considerably, and the reader who stays by the poet's side discovers that he is alternately inside and outside the work. Practically all the poems have at least the value of a pleasant decoration; some probe beneath the surface, and in these the reader takes the initial steps with the artist in his poetic quest. For the reader who knows all the work of EGM, the particular charm of this first volume is its reflection of *modernismo*.

A high degree of sophistication is the keynote of "Laugh" ("Ríe"), in which the poet addresses a salon goddess. We have already seen part of its opening lines, "Loose, fair goddess, the cascade/ of your golden laughter" (*Suelta, divina rubia, la cascada/ de tu risa de oro*). (I.10) The poet prepares the reader through synesthetic association in these first lines to enjoy a sensual experience. He also suggests an elegant woman with the use of "fair goddess." Then he indicates the feminine ambivalence by referring to the "satanic sparkle" (*destello satánico*) of her eyes. So it is that in the first stanza the reader finds himself observing a well-known *modernista* charmer, gay, seductive, teasing, and probably cruel.

There is enough of the pastoral tradition—the drawing-room pastoral, that is—in the poetry of EGM's early period to make this initial scene a perfectly natural one for salon, garden, or wood. But the second stanza fixes the scene inside (or in a garden), not by definite statement, but by reference to champagne and orchestra. The poet uses both elements to heighten the synesthetic effect: both are laughing and both are used to suggest color. The champagne easily suggests gold, and the poet supplies "silvery" (*argentina*) to describe the laughter of the orchestra. This laughter, incidentally, is not a simple *risa* but a *carcajada*, a *burst* of laughter. And the burst of laughter is the laughter of love, an association that increases the erotic sense of the poem and at the same time—through the quality of the laughter—links love to the devilish quality of the woman.

In the two following stanzas, the poet interrupts the feeling of being in the woman's immediate presence by informing her of what she must already know, obviously addressing her from a distance. The reader steps out of the scene, and hears of her gaiety, her ignorance of suffering. While this digression does tend toward the contemplative, its imagery maintains the poem's atmosphere of luxury. In the last two stanzas, EGM brings the reader back into the immediate presence, beginning each stanza with the exhortation "Drink." (I.10) The images again suggest bubbling happiness, party laughter, mild drunkenness. At the end of the poem, the poet enters the action as he exhorts her, when he kisses her shoulder, to burst out laughing "like a shower of gold" (*como una lluvia de oro*). (I.11) The last stanza recalls the imagery of the first, retains the established synesthesia, but intensifies the scene through the participation of the poet and by changing the woman's laughter from *risa* to *carcajada*. And as the poem is thus intensified, the reader's feeling of being in the immediate presence is strengthened.

Beneath the feeling of charming madness that EGM gives his reader in this poem, there is also a feeling of lack of completeness, or lack of fulfillment. We feel that we must go on being tantalized and still be forever left alone. A similar feeling of reaching out is in "Al amor" ("To Love"), a poem which is more dependent on mythology and which we observe rather than experience in the sense of feeling a part of the scene. We do, however, participate in the poetic moment because EGM draws us into his contemplation. Through the use of mythological allusions and very precious language, the artist establishes the poem quite apart from worldly reality. The scene is static except for the radiation of beauty from the statuesque woman. The cruelty of the unresponsive beloved is made clear by reference to her, in the first stanza, as "the one who is my torment" (*la que es tormento mío*) (I.12) and, near the end of the poem, when the agonized lover would have Love's arrow bring about "her punishment and my vengeance." (I.12) In spite of the use of colors which tend to make the beloved come alive, her unresponsive, statuesque quality, suggested early in the poem by comparison to a Greek vase, becomes absolute at the end, when the lover is resigned to the fact that the arrow will be blunted against marble. EGM develops the poem in such a way that a flesh-and-blood woman is a possibility at the beginning, but that possibility is transformed definitively into statue. What was a possible response at the start terminates in marble silence. We are left alone, much as if newly-found friends had deserted us after an initial cordial greeting.

The best known poem of *Preludios* is "Rústica" ("Peasant Girl"), which is not a single poem but a series of fourteen related sonnets. Together they tell a story of a young country girl, Casta (Chastity), who has her initial sexual experience with a rustic lad who has been waiting for his opportunity. But "Peasant Girl" is no sordid story of seduction. The poet combines sexuality with nature in such a way that they are one and the same thing. Here the poet's creative seeking takes us toward the innocence of humanity in an uncomplicated society. Indeed, the twelfth sonnet, "Paréntesis," leaves the development of the "plot" so the poet can inform the city girl (the characterization of "Laugh") that her coquetry is really of little consequence, that the peasant is as noble as the oak, and that his sexual instinct is the same as an animal's. In fairness to the poet, it should be stated here that talking about what he says is a little absurd. Obviously, his poem says much more than an account of it could communicate. We can only state the theme.

While the sonnet series is narrative, it is more like a collection of sequential slides than like a movie. Each of the sonnets is improved by being part of the whole, but any one of them will stand on its own. The first one, "Preludio," is a mood setting for the series. EGM captures the feeling of the edge of dawn in a hazy word picture that is very typical of *modernismo*: "the sad, misty distance," "the tenuous clarity of day," "a vague resplendence." (I. 29) Then he relates the awakening of the day to the sexual awakening of the girl. The description of the full brilliance of dawn, in the second sonnet, implies a corresponding intensity in the girl's sexual awareness. Following an orderly development of the story, the author describes the rural scene in the third sonnet, and Casta herself in the fourth. The pastoral quality of these sonnets is not uncommon, and is much like the effect of the poetry of Julio Herrera y Reissig and some of Leopoldo Lugones'. The countryside and, indeed, Casta herself, are too perfectly beautiful to be real, yet they are alive. They are idealizations, but they are idealizations that require the suspension of humdrum ugliness, not the suspension of breathing or of the heartbeat. They are unreal only because peasants and the rural landscape are not as close to primitive innocence as the poet would like to believe.

Subsequent sonnets join Casta with nature, and in the seventh, the second actor is introduced as if he were a part of nature. Then the poet develops the eroticism of the lovers and of nature, emphasizes its instinctive quality by joining them. After the parenthesis addressed to the city girl, the poet informs us, through the symbol of Casta's broken water jug, that her name is less appropriate than it was at the start; or better said, she has lost her innocence in terms of sophisticated society, but on her own terms there is hardly a question of innocence and guilt. Her resistance and her surrender have been of equal intensity; and though she has a certain feeling of defeat, her principal reaction is resignation. Woman here is to an extent the antagonist, but she is also the promise of the answer to the question. Even if "Peasant Girl" gives us no more than the promise, the poet has carried his search farther than in "Laugh" or in "To Love." It is of considerable importance that the more developed feeling of certainty that comes from "Peasant Girl" is produced by the association of human instinct with nature. The fact suggests a major thread in the fabric of EGM's work.

Long before González Martínez advocated wringing the swan's neck, he had addressed the poet in terms that certainly foreshadow his famous exhortation. "To a Poet" ("A un poeta") is not one of the most successful pieces in *Preludios*, but it is another indication of his working his way through to his own expression, and a very clear indication of the route he would take.

> Where did you learn the sickly song
> that you broadcast like a moribund swan?
> Who speaks—tell me—of dying so long
> as the sun, the sacred sun, fires the world?
>
> .   .   .   .
>
> Look at the field, observe the sea, consider the sky:
> there you find beauty, inspiration, everything!
>
> (*¿Dónde aprendiste el enfermizo canto
> que lanzas como cisne moribundo?
> ¿Quién habla—dime—de morir en tanto
> que el sol, el almo sol, incendia el mundo?*
>
> .   .   .   .
>
> *¡Ve el campo, mira el mar, contempla el cielo:
> allí hay belleza, inspiración y todo!*)[8]

The poem consists of thirteen quatrains, and the quotation is the second and part of the fourth. EGM used this first portion of the poem to state his proposition; the following verses are descriptions of aspects of nature. They amount to a cataloguing rather than a development, but they are notable for two reasons: the presence of a wide variety of the things of nature, and the feeling of genuine nature that is different from the artificiality of nature in some of the other early poems.

III   *The Short Stories*

The consideration of EGM's prose fiction constitutes no more than a parenthesis in the study of his work. He did try his hand at several literary genres in the early years, but was satisfied only with poetry. Most of his other work was not published; and of the pieces that were published, only a few have been collected. The only stories that are readily available are two that were published in a selection of his prose made by Ana María Sánchez.[9] These stories indicate that EGM could have been a successful writer of prose fiction, and they reveal a few points of contact with his poetry. But they also show why the author chose not to continue writing in prose, because it is quite obvious that these short stories did not offer him the opportunity for open-ended communication that he found in poetry. The stories are too definitive, too much the illustration of his point, when they are compared to poetry which by its power of suggestion enables both poet and reader to understand more deeply than is possible through the severely rational understanding of a prose statement.

The earlier of the two stories, "A Female" ("Una hembra"), turns on the strength of the maternal instinct. The protagonist's values are changed radically when she becomes a mother. She is a woman of the lower class, economically, and it is important that the author finds in her a natural goodness that he appears to find generally in simpler people. We might reasonably debate whether the author understands this goodness as existing because of or in spite of her social condition. But there is no doubt that the change brought about by the birth of her child reflects the author's faith in the positive force of creativity.

Technically, the story is almost a definition of Realism, but without dialogue. It begins with a description of the protagonist and then moves to the events. Each character is introduced before he does anything. The omniscient author tells us what each one is like, and little or nothing is added to the characterization in any other way. The development is lineal and is divided into three parts to allow for the passage of time. The style is pleasant and employs some imagery, but it is mainly simple description.

"The Little Girl" ("La chiquilla") shows considerably more sophistication in the art of story writing. The point of the story is that the little girl who is the protagonist is not so little any more. She has reached puberty and is, as a matter of fact, a small-town version of Casta, the country girl of *Preludios*. She is the ward of a priest, the daughter of a prostitute. EGM allows her unfortunate background to suggest to the reader that she may be headed in the same direction; but the suggestion is a false alarm, because the author is really concerned with the natural reality of her instinct, just as he was concerned with the basic maternal instinct in "A Female."

The content of the story reveals the priest's awareness of his ward's need for longer dresses, and through the action justifies

his opinion. Actually what happens is that the girl does a sort
of striptease (described in detail by the author) in the privacy
of her room, *but* when she knows the sacristan is watching
through the keyhole. Her controlled desire to laugh during this
episode identifies her with the tantalizing woman of the poems.
Her emotion is the climax and end of the story and the author
builds up to it very skillfully. He sets the scene by description
of the ambitious but mediocre priest, finding him in his study
where he is interrupted by the girl. Her past is explained in a
flashback, and then the story proceeds. The circumstances of
the story offer more possibilities than in "A Female": we wonder
about the girl's background, and we also wonder what effect
her intense femininity will have on the priest. The author dis-
cards these possibilities gracefully in a prose style that is clear
and unobtrusive. His attitude toward the circumstance gives
the story a light, gently humorous charm, but we know that his
basic intent was to present one view of eternal woman. The
story is Realistic although it has some overtones of *modernismo*
in its insistence on the feminine constant and the rather poetic
description of the striptease.

One further point of contact may be seen between this
story and EGM's poetry. He has a tendency in both to humanize
men of the church; that is, he tends to set them on the ground
rather than on a pedestal, but not with any bitterness. This
view of the clergy is not a prominent theme in his work, but
it may contribute to the understanding of the poet's religious
experience which appears to transcend any organized expression
of the sacred. However, this similarity, like others already mentioned, does not really add anything to the appreciation of
EGM's poetry. They emphasize some of his attitudes, and they
show that he could write stories but chose what was for him
the less limited medium of poetry.

IV Lirismos

Lirismos, which was published in 1907, four years after *Preludios*, is a much smaller collection and is composed almost
entirely of sonnets. González Martínez continued to improve
as a craftsman of verse, but the truth is that we rarely think of
form when we read him. He was so very competent that his
form never intrudes except in the few cases where he is experi-

menting or where he employs a sudden change for the sake of
effective communication. Antonio Castro Leal, the eminent Mexican critic who sees as clearly as anyone the influences on EGM,
notes some subtle changes between the first and second volumes
of poetry.[10] He supposes a basic influence of Horace ("To Love"
is an example) and sees the clearest Mexican influences as
Salvador Díaz Mirón and Joaquín Arcadio Pagaza. These more
recent poets were landscapists, and we might suppose another
more distant influence of Virgil, especially in poems like "Peasant
Girl." Castro Leal sees these influences as greatly diminished
in the second volume of poetry, and recognizes the stronger
influence of the French poets whom EGM was reading and
translating. He also notes that the poet frequently forsakes the
objectivity of the French parnassians. It is on these occasions
that we appreciate EGM's progress toward the discovery of his
own poetic voice.

The extent to which the poet's individuality enters his work
varies a good deal from poem to poem. It should be clearly
understood that this factor does not necessarily control the value
of the poem; rather, it changes the means of communication.
And this means, in EGM's best poems, does provide added
depth—or perhaps it would be more accurate to say "added
reach."

In "Evocation" ("Evocación"), the poet establishes a contrast
between the feeling of the sonnet's octave and that of its sextet.
The octave is tropical and everything is very much alive. Nature
is personified. At the beginning of the sextet, his thoughts turn
to an unidentified "you" (he uses the familiar address). With
this change of mental focus, the poem becomes arctic, colorless,
and virtually lifeless. In the largest sense, this sonnet is a contrast between life and death, though it should not be inferred
that the poet is addressing the Grim Reaper. It is clear that
the reference is to someone whose position the poet respects:
"you who reign among the mists" ("la que reinas entre las
brumas.") (I.1) He could indeed be addressing death as a
queen, or the "you" could be the unresponsive beloved—certainly
the glacial quality of the sextet indicates lack of response. Whatever the identification of the "you"—and a specific identity would
be absurd—the point and the feeling of the poem are that there
is a barrier to carrying out life, and here is a lack of fulfillment
very similar to the feeling of several poems in *Preludios.* "Evoca-

tion" is extremely effective in communicating the feeling because the contrast is so clear, and the transition so smooth.

"Hidden Spring" ("Fuente oculta")[11] increases our awareness of the poet's sensitivity to nature which we glimpsed in "To a Poet." Here the door is opened a bit wider and we feel the profound respect that the poet shows for innocence. The first quatrain of this sonnet contains the line "the silvery falling of your diaphanous drops" that we have already considered. In the same stanza (the poet is actually addressing the spring), we know that this is an isolated scene, an expression of life in solitude. It is only on second thought that the choice of running water as an expression of life seems in any way strange. The virgin quality of the spring—it is unseen, unspoiled—becomes the theme of the second stanza, and its innocence is so perfect that it knows nothing of its own origin. The first tercet is a hope for its continued innocence, and the last is the poet's apology for intruding. Here is EGM's exquisite sensitivity to innocence and to silence.

> Pardon if for a moment my indiscreet glance
> surprised unwittingly your secret existence . . .
> And allow me to depart with silent step.
>
> *(Perdona si un instante mi indiscreta mirada*
> *sorprendió, sin quererlo, tu existencia ignorada . . .*
> *Y déjame alejarme con silencioso paso.)* (I.2)

The association of water with innocence is a growing discovery in the poetry of González Martínez, and it eventually accents the primordial condition so that innocence and perfection become one. Indeed, the sea finally expresses this knowledge; but EGM's relationship with the sea was a long one, and what he saw through it changed with passing time and broadening vision. "Facing the Sea" ("Frente al mar") is probably his first poem in which the subject appears. The poet had always wanted to view the sea, and he did so for the first time when he moved with his parents and sister to Sinaloa. In this sonnet the poet occupies the center of the stage and we stand with him, viewing the awesome spectacle, sharing his emotional reaction. We are before the "sleepless quiet of the shore" (*insomne quietud de la ribera*) (I.3) and enveloped "in the monotonous and savage sadness" (*en la tristeza monótona y salvaje*). (I.3) The passage of a bird completes the picture. In the second stanza the poet introduces the yearning for distant lands, which here is a reaching out in the abstract, not toward any specific place. In the sextet, addressing the sea, he observes that while no one has ever taken leave of him by sea, he still feels that its waves are taking something away from him.

There is one further note in *Lirismos* that deserves attention as an indication of the nature of the poet's quest. "Berceuse" is, of course, a lullaby. The poet wrote it for his infant son, Jorge, and the sonnet simply wishes him a meaningful and happy life. An allegory of a boat sailing through life is constant throughout the poem. It is musical, peaceful, loving, and unpretentious. Still the self-revelation of the poet in the first two lines is worth consideration:

> May your life glide like a small boat
> over the gentle current, quiet and mysterious, . . .
>
> *(Deslícese tu vida como una barquichuela*
> *sobre corriente mansa, callada y misteriosa, . . .* (I.26)

It is difficult for one who has read the later poetry of EGM to guess how much these lines say to a reader who has not had that experience. The lines suggest what is probably an unrealistically smooth journey, but this is obviously a concept of life in movement; and the poet's life was one of movement in the awareness of things, rather than an unexpectant waiting. Yet, the movement is quiet, and so it is with EGM. We may recall his reaction in "Hidden Spring." Life moves with awareness, but awareness requires a certain deliberation, a kind of dignity, and it moves quietly because it is expectant, listening. And of course it is mysterious. The searching is not for a definite thing, but for what life offers, which can be received only in quietness, in dignity. Whatever it is that the sea sends back to us, in response to what goes out from us, can be ours only if we maintain the integrity of the silent search.

V Silénter

It was while González Martínez was preparing the poems of *Silénter* (1909) for publication that he seemed to hear his own voice for the first time. There was ample reason for this feeling because, in this third volume of poetry, the artist is much more attentive to the poetic inclinations that were peculiarly his own.

Silénter does not represent a violent break in the development
of his poetry, but a changing emphasis is very apparent. If "The
Centauress" ("La centauresa") and some other poems of this
volume clearly recall the earlier work, "You Will Pass Over the
Life of Things" ("Irás sobre la vida de las cosas") and a number
of others even more clearly mark the new emphasis which came
with the poet's discovery of his authentic voice.

"The Centauress" is an erotic poem, rich with *modernista*
coloring, that moves in a mythological world which, in spite of
its unreality, communicates a strong feeling of natural purity.
The very irreality of it suggests the search for something that is
not ordinarily obtainable. We feel a strong attachment to the
mythological world in "Dead Gods" ("Dioses muertos"), where
EGM appears to regret not being able to stay within the world
that had inspired much of his poetry. This sonnet refers to the
savage silence of natural surroundings that we have found in
other poems, and also to the same eroticism. Here the reader
feels that EGM may have certain regrets about his new poetic
road; and it is also possible that he is sensitive to the difficulty
he would always have in reconciling the so-called rational world
with the poetic one. His mythological world is a clearer escape
from the muddle of humanity than is his journey over the life
of things. The latter route often left him suspended between
the world and the heights, sometimes fearful of the abyss, sometimes feeling that he should be more strongly committed to it.

"Since the Boat Is Mine" ("Como la barca es mía") is a kind
of declaration of poetic independence. The poet will go where
he wishes, and he senses how wide the world is—not just the
geographical world, but the whole poetic reality of all that exists
and can be created. After establishing this ebullient freedom
in the sonnet's octave, EGM uses the sextet in a more specific
way, informing an unidentified "you" that he will not be stopped.
We have the feeling of a lonely but satisfying adventure, and a
certain satisfaction in being able to withdraw from what we
ordinarily consider the world. This is the assertion of poetic
freedom that will save him from the fate of Baudelaire's alba-
tross.

"Vivere vitam" is to some extent complementary to "Since the
Boat Is Mine," because it intensifies the joyful feeling of the
latter. Indeed, "Vivere vitam" communicates a live-for-today
attitude that sounds a little strange in EGM's poetry. Although

he certainly believed in living life fully, the living was not usually in terms of such worldly joys. Here, instead of withdrawing from the muddled throng, he advocates taking advantage of all the pleasures that the world offers with the knowledge that later on, if he wishes, he may take the "hidden path": "Never deny your lips to the lighted flower/of a thirsting mouth." (I.54) The tone is one of exhortation, and it begins as if it were a reply to someone who had just expressed the opposite feeling. It would seem that the poet is addressing himself and is sensing his way to a decision. Certainly his reader is on both sides at once.

The key poem of this collection is undoubtedly "You Will Pass Over the Life of Things." The poem is written in six quatrains that are as economical as a sonnet, and in them EGM clarifies the nature of the poetic quest and of the reunion of the poet with all creation. The first verb of the poem, which is also in the title, is in the future tense, and it lends a gentle note of certainty to the less forceful subjunctives of the verbs that follow. After the statement—perhaps the prophecy—that "you will pass over the life of things," the poet continues with hopeful expressions that can best be given in English as "may you." The use of the second person may be taken as the poet's hope for someone else, but it also appears that the poet, in some way apart from himself, addresses himself as in "Vivere vitam." Certainly through the use of this address, and through development of a sense of present moving into future, the poem captures the reader and he too lives expectantly in the possibility of seeing always more deeply.

It must be noted that our passage over the life of things will not be hurried, but will be with a "noble slowness" (*noble lentitud*). (I.49) The passage is not free; it demands attention, dignity, respect. Finishing the first stanza we anticipate communication with everything because the poet reinforces his reference to "all" by listing the white, blue, and red of snow, water, and roses. We have a feeling of all things united in color. In the second stanza we can expect that everything will leave its imprint on us, and this imprint becomes stronger later in the poem because things actually become a part of us. But in the second stanza the expression is less intense—we know only that we should receive the effect of things. In the same stanza, the universality of our communication is emphasized by reference to the spring, or fountain, and the star—one distant, the other close by. Now the two stanzas have used both color and space to produce the feeling of "allness."

In the third stanza we glimpse the possibility of ascent. The heights, the peaks, the mountain, always mean the inspiring struggle to grasp the secret of life in EGM's poetry. On the heights we will be responsive to the wind. Then follows a stanza that must be seen in its entirety:

> May you avoid what confuses and what astonishes
> the human flock that remains below,
> and may you tune your soul until it can
> hear the silence and see the darkness.

> *(Que esquives lo que ofusca y lo que asombra*
> *al humano redil que abajo queda,*
> *y que afines tu alma hasta que pueda*
> *escuchar el silencio y ver la sombra.)* (I.49)

The first two lines of the stanza certainly indicate that we are looking for a very special knowing, one that is not available to those who will not ascend. The reference to human beings as a "flock" has a pejorative connotation and reflects the poet's reluctance to stay below. It is not that he flatly condemns people as such, but that he despises their lack of desire to know, to ascend. There is something about society that limits the vision of its individual components, and we must avoid this phenomenon if we want to ascend. The last two lines of the stanza describe the sensitivity that we must develop in order to realize the communication that we seek. The acts that are described, since they are impossible in the ordinary sense, identify the nature of the quest.

The intensity of the fifth stanza brings the whole poem to a climax as both present search and future discovery are concentrated in the individual:

> May you love yourself within yourself, your
> being synthesizing heavens and abyss, so that
> without ceasing to look at yourself,
> your eyes may contemplate everything.

> *(Que te ames en ti mismo, de tal modo*
> *compendiando tu ser cielo y abismo,*
> *que sin desviar los ojos de ti mismo*
> *puedan tus ojos contemplarlo todo.)* (I.50)

This is the moment of complete reunion, not exactly experienced but felt through intense anticipation. The individual's movement between the heights and the abyss is halted in this supreme moment of synthesis when the two extremes are joined in a perfect wholeness. This moment is not often realized in EGM's poetry. Vertical movement is frequently present, but usually we either follow it from one extreme to the other, or find ourselves suspended in between. The feeling of synthesis remains one of anticipation. But here, briefly, anticipation is so intense that it is hardly distinguished from reality. The state of wholeness is described in the last stanza as a "minute universe" (*minúsculo universo*). (I.50) With his minute universe, the poet may come to the "hidden shore," (I.50) another expression which suggests reaching out, being on the brink of knowing the great secret. And the anticipation is that there the poet may hear his own verse "in which the soul of life beats" (*en que palpita el alma de la vida*). (I.50) Here then is another union created by the poet's having absorbed so much of life that his song and life are equal to each other.

Anticipation becomes realization in "Sometimes a Fallen Leaf" ("A veces una hoja desprendida"). Here the poet addresses no one—he is talking about what happens to him—yet through the feeling of actuality, the reader joins the writer's experience. He is contemplative, and mildly astonished at the impact of what happens.

> At times, a leaf fallen
> from high up in the trees, a sighing
> of passing waters, a sonorous
> nightingale trill, upset my life.
>
> (*A veces, una hoja desprendida*
> *de lo alto de los árboles, un lloro*
> *de las linfas que pasan, un sonoro*
> *trino de ruiseñor, turban mi vida.*) (I.52)

The intensity of the moment created in this stanza comes mainly from the relationship of the end of one line to the beginning of the following (*enjambement*). This technique is made even stronger by rhyme in the Spanish, and it concentrates the presence of things at the moment when they affect the poet. He says that he has this awareness "sometimes," not that he has cultivated it so that it is constant. In four following stanzas, he uses other things to create four similar moments. And then in the sixth, in an exultant burst, he exclaims:

> Divine communion! . . . For an instant
> my senses have a rare sharpness . . .
>
> (*¡ Divina comunión! . . . Por un instante*
> *son mis sentidos de agudeza rara . . .*) (I.53)

This is the poet's reaction to the miracle of having experienced the resplendent moment when the full reality of something is apparent. This is the moment when something whose reality we take for granted, suddenly becomes more than what we have known it to be previously. EGM *creates* the moment more successfully in some other poems than he does in "Sometimes a Fallen Leaf," but he never *describes* it more clearly than here. The following stanza is a statement of what happens to him:

> I free myself from everything and I disassociate myself
> to live a new life in such a way
> that I do not know whether I become a part of everything
> or everything enters into me and goes with me.
>
> (*De todo me liberto y me desligo*
> *a vivir nueva vida, de tal modo,*
> *que yo no sé si me difundo en todo*
> *o todo me penetra y va conmigo.*) (I.53)

Subsequently, the poet explains that the new reality escapes him and his pursuing soul is left in loneliness. That is why he listens so attentively to nature. He awaits the return of the resplendent moment. The last stanza of the poem is a repetition of the first, so the poet's contemplation of the moment is framed by the words through which he comes closest, in this poem, to creating the moment itself. We are left with a feeling of a never-ending cycle of anticipation, realization, and loss.

Even within the magic of the resplendent moment, EGM is sometimes aware of the possibility of knowing even beyond that point. The sonnet "In a Low Voice" ("En voz baja") discusses or describes the moment in a way similar to the structure of "Sometimes a Fallen Leaf." The first quatrain and part of the second build the feeling of profound communion; then suddenly, the relationship is lost. In expressing the sense of loss, the poet shifts from the imagery of voice and hearing as the basis of communication, and uses the concept of unrequited love. The change in imagery makes a good transition into the sextet, where the poet follows "you," referring to nature on the most obvious level but at the same time extending to the great secret that is ultimate knowing. When he says "Hermetic, you hide from me the key to the secret" (*Hermética me escondes la clave del arcano*), (I.67) he seems to be seeking something more than what he has already experienced. This feeling is enhanced by the effect of the word *arcano* which derives from a word that means "chest"—it is a little different from *secreto*, which also appears in this sonnet. In the last tercet, he combines voice-hearing imagery with love imagery, and asks a question as if he were indeed talking to the beloved, wondering when she will reveal the secret to him.

The use of the poetic voice is not always satisfactory. The will to create the resplendent moment does not always bring success. In "I Dreamed of a Verse" ("Soñé en un verso"), the poet uses the octave to speak of a "vibrant verse" (I.57) that he would like to write. He by no means writes the verse, but suggests the brilliance it would have, and the way it would incorporate what he senses in nature. But the sextet describes the quality of the verse that he really makes: melancholy, soft, muted, imprisoned in shadow. This final description carries the feeling of the poet's not being able to say all he feels because it will not come clearly in words. At times we feel that the poet anticipates knowledge that transcends even the revelation of the resplendent moment; but it may be that his feeling unfulfilled comes not from the expectation of further knowing, but from the need to create the moment itself.

González Martínez sometimes uses nature simply as a backdrop for contemplation, as in "Solitude" ("Soledad"). Here he allows himself more liberty of form than is generally found in his early poetry, and it is very appropriate in this case because he is letting his thoughts drift. There is no hint of divine communication in this poem. The artist is very aware of nature and paints it in beautiful imagery, but it is not united with him. It provides a refuge where he can meditate, removed from worldly confusion. And meditation is essential in a poetic process where there is conflict between commitment to ordinary life and commitment to the act of ascending. In "Pity" ("Piedad"), the poet expresses the impossibility of resolving the conflict. The sonnet's octave shows the necessity of disregarding those who remain below in the human muddle, but the sextet shows the insistence of pity. The conflict haunts EGM, and it haunts his reader. The synthesis reached in the development of "You Will Pass Over the Life of Things" is rarely attainable. "La-haut" creates the desperate difficulty of the ascent, not only because the climbing is difficult, but also because the fall is easy. There is an end to the fall, an end that promises rest, but the ascent goes on forever, "and when you raise your eyes you see the stars as far away as ever." (I.44)

The striving, the reaching, the constant climbing in search of clarity, it seems, is more than another way of expressing the reunion achieved within the resplendent moment. It is a challenge to the moment itself. And it is also a confession that the ultimate has to be ultimate in fact. Facing this reality, Enrique González Martínez found his poetic road.

CHAPTER 2

The Poet's Universe

And may you come at last
to the secret shore with
your minute universe . . .—
"You will Pass Over the
Life of Things"

I The Hidden Paths

IF *Silénter* leaves any doubt about the new direction of EGM's
poetry, it is dispelled by "Muse" ("Musa"), the first poem
in *The Hidden Paths* (*Los senderos ocultos*), 1911. Identifying
his muse as a "female satyr" (*satiresa*), (I.107) the poet creates
the feeling of his earlier work. After five quatrains, he begins
to develop the transition that is started by a deeper awareness
of reality: "But from then on, the frisky beast/ changed both
direction and doctrine" (*Mas desde entonces la locuela/ cambió
de rumbo y de doctrina*). (I.108) In the next stanza, the state
of his muse is clearly related to the poet's new attitude:

> On the threshold of madness,
> strange symbol, she clings to
> the earth with her hoofs
> and to the heights with her eyes.
>
> (*En el umbral de la locura,
> extraño símbolo, se aferra
> con las pesuñas a la tierra,
> con las pupilas a la altura.*) (I.108)

The duality of allegiance, or of commitment, that we see in
this stanza is a problem that appears throughout EGM's poetry,
often created in a pendulum-like emotional uncertainty.

We are able to see now some of the main lines of the poet's
creative weaving, basing our understanding on what we have
already seen, and perhaps unavoidably anticipating a bit of
42

what we may expect. The most important thread is the desire for reunion with all creation, a state that the poet explains, anticipates, or realizes, depending on the characteristics of the particular poem. This quest for reunion is the source of a great many of the resplendent moments when, through the poetic act, the artist—and the reader, if he is fully attuned to the poetry—discovers reality that cannot be expressed in rational terms, but can only be known through the effect of the creative process. The desire for reunion presupposes a state of wholeness from which the poet is separated. Even when he does not achieve reunion through the creative process, the poet may approximate that splendid reality through a more limited sort of communication. There are times, however, when the reality of separation dominates the reality of reunion. Then the poet is in solitude, and he experiences sorrow. But solitude has two other meanings in EGM's poetry. First, it is a state in which we find ourselves when the pendulum swings toward the heights, or when we ascend. The wonderful effect of this solitude is mitigated by the commitment to earth where the human muddle inhibits the poetic quest. The other solitude is one that the poet seeks deliberately and physically, for the purpose of contemplation. These two kinds of solitude are not always independent of each other.

Solitude is different from silence which is one of the requirements for seeking reunion. The latter is a symbol of the respect with which we approach creation in expectation of reunion. EGM uses many different ways of referring to this approach, most of them characterized by some expression like "profound" which suggests going beyond what we usually experience. We find also that there are limits to knowing. Even though we may experience the resplendent moment, our knowing is limited—perhaps because we cannot maintain the moment, perhaps because we sense the eternal secret even beyond the resplendent moment. Since the limit to knowing is present in one way or the other, the search for the final answer must go on indefinitely. This uncertainty brings up questions about the properties of death or the continuity of life. They are not answered on their own terms, and so it is not possible to speak of a specific attitude toward death in EGM's poetry. But participating with the poet, we do round the circle in our consideration of his weaving, and return to the desire for reunion with creation.

Insofar as a volume of poetry can be described in a few words, *The Hidden Paths* is an implementation of EGM's ideas concerning the profound search. It is, at the same time, a continuing discovery of the meaning of the search, through varied statements that contribute to the perspective in which it is seen. This discovery of meaning goes back as far as "To a Poet," from EGM's first volume. In its pursuit, the poet sometimes captures the resplendent moment, sometimes he addresses himself as a means of capturing it. In some poems, his anxiety reaches such intensity that he appears to be exhorting others, excluding himself, like some sort of evangelist of the poetic search. The knotting of this particular thread is found in "Wring the Swan's Neck," not because this poem says anything radically different from what can be found in other poems by EGM, but because he mentions the swan, a symbol of *modernismo* in general and of Rubén Darío in particular.

"Seek in All Things" ("Busca en todas las cosas") is a clear statement of the theme of "Wring the Swan's Neck." It is written in seven quatrains and is somewhat less economical than the famous sonnet, but the call to the profound search is unmistakable.

> Seek in all things a soul and a hidden
> meaning; be not bound to vain appearance;
> smell out, follow the trail of the secret truth
> with searching eye and attentive ear.
>
> (*Busca en todas las cosas un alma y un sentido*
> *oculto; no te ciñas a la apariencia vana;*
> *husmea, sigue el rastro de la verdad arcana,*
> *escudriñante el ojo y aguzado el oído.*) (I.110)

The poet does not specifically mention form and language here as he does in "Wring the Swan's Neck," but there is no doubt that he refers to the poetic act in both pieces. "Seek in All Things" also refers again to the sensitivity of eye and ear, so vividly created in "You Will Pass Over the Life of Things" where we anticipate hearing silence and seeing shadow. The particular dimension that "Seek in All Things" adds to our awareness of the depth of the search is found in the second stanza. Here we appreciate the possibility of knowing what might be called a pre-existent reality—the awareness of something before it *is*.

> Be not like the fool who, when he sees the virginal
> imperfection of the marble imprisoned in clay,
> is deaf to the heart of the stone that intones,
> in a recondite rhythm, the song of its line.

> (*No seas como el necio, que al mirar la virgínea
> imperfección del mármol que la arcilla aprisiona,
> queda sordo a la entraña de la piedra, que entona
> en recóndito ritmo, la canción de la línea.*) (I.110)

This concept is one of several that EGM uses to create a sense of "further reality." It is more than an acute response of the senses; rather, it is an entirely different response, like hearing silence.

"I Offer to Life the Supplication" ("Tiendo a la vida el ruego") moves from self-analysis to confident expectation. In the beginning, we have a feeling of humility before the vastness of life, and the humility is intensified by acknowledgment of the desire for complete reunion. The poet uses the figure of a beggar asking alms, then his mood of self-analysis inspires a parenthetical confession that the poet, unlike the beggar, wants all. He then describes the change in his poetic point of view that we have already seen in "Muse." In the next two lines EGM brings more insight into the desire for reunion, intensifying it and making it complete to a degree that will be sensed again in other poems. If a bird, singing, should enter his consciousness, he says, "I would like to be at once both bird and song" (*quisiera ser a un tiempo el pájaro y el trino*). (I.140) The main significance of the line in the context of this poem is the contribution to the sense of wholeness of life that is made by insistence on both bird *and* song. But we do not lose the effect of *be*. He does not speak of hearing or of seeing, but of being; and by expressing the feeling this way, the poem enlarges the possibilities suggested by the very special and profound sense responses. It is specifically this line that moves us into the vibrant expectation of the rest of the poem, where we feel not only the magic of potential reunion, but the confidence that it will be realized.

More expectation and much of the feeling of "You Will Pass Over the Life of Things" come alive in "When You Know How to Find a Smile" ("Cuando sepas hallar una sonrisa"). This is a poem in seven quatrains with a very effectively balanced structure. The first three stanzas all begin with "when" and they create the state of receptivity that we seek, reaching the culmination in the last lines of the third stanza, when our striving will "be like a powerful microscope/ that discovers invisible universes" (*"sea como potente microscopio/ que va hallando invisibles universos"*). (I.128) The fourth stanza is the fulcrum which the first set of three uses to propel the final set of three into high expectation. It begins with "then" and switches from the subjunctive to the more positive future tense. It communicates reunion, not in the form of an amorphous body but in the brotherhood of individuals. In this transitional stanza and in the preceding three, the anticipated relationship has mainly suggested communication with *things*: the anticipation is that we will find a smile in a drop of water, in the mist, in the sun, in the breeze—and in a bird, the only item in the list that is animate in the usual sense of the word. Actually, the smile has a transfer value in this figure, because it applies to the seeker, or to the anticipated relationship, rather than to the object. That is, the smile helps to identify the relationship. In the fifth stanza (the first of the set of three that counterpoints the first three), things are joined with beings.

> You will sense your own being in the
> immense multitude of beings and things;
>
> (*Sentirás en la inmensa muchedumbre*
> *de seres y cosas tu sér mismo;*) (I.129)

Immediately after these lines, we are aware of the vertical movement, and find ourselves in the midst of the conflict between abyss and heights.

All three of the final stanzas continue in the future tense, each beginning with a verb and emphasizing the promise. The poet uses the "you" form and gives the poem a tone very similar to that of "You Will Pass Over the Life of Things." This address is much safer for the poet's intent than the imperative that he uses in some instances. "Seek in All Things" is dangerously authoritative in tone. If it were not for the fact that the depth of the search assures us that the imperative applies to the author as much as to anyone else, the reader would probably become detached from the process. The future tense is far more positive and very much more encompassing.

The kind of knowing that is the product of the profound search is accompanied by silence, and is available only with silence. If there were not silence, the communication would be impossible; and silence also signifies an individual integrity that corresponds to the wholeness of creation. "Psalle et sile"[1] is a bidding to silence that clearly includes the poet himself as well as others. The first statement of the poem uses the infinitive rather than the imperative, and although the poet later switches to the imperative, its force is mitigated by the generality of the infinitive. So the feeling of the poem is one of growing sensitivity to what we ought to do, rather than of being lectured on a set of principles. This poem may be taken too superficially by readers who are not within it, for it lends itself to an easy misinterpretation of gentle stoicism. A deeper reading creates the feeling of the integrity of life—not the activity in the human muddle, but life as it relates to being. And the suggestion is not that we should not weep, but rather that we should, if it is necessary; however, the weeping itself should have a special quality, like that of the hidden spring. We know that the spring is a part of creation and that it is also a source. Our weeping, then, takes on a creative characteristic and becomes part of the endless quest. But since the quest must be a silent one, so also the weeping must be quiet.

The development of the poem is effected through images that suggest ascent and communication. Life does indeed contain sadness as well as joy—and here we feel very briefly the pendulum movement, as if we were swinging toward worldly confusion—but each emotion must become a part of our being. Our being is joined with life, and that is why we must respect its integrity. EGM frames the poem by repeating the opening lines at the end.

"Wring the Swan's Neck" comes as something of an anticlimax to the reader who has been with the poet from the beginning of this volume. Still, since it is undoubtedly the most quoted and most discussed of all of EGM's poetry, it tends to become the central poem. And we should be perfectly clear about this: it is a fine sonnet and communicates a feeling similar to that found in a number of his other poems and is quite consistent with the general development of his work. The poet himself called special attention to it by referring to it in the title of his next volume. Many critics consider it the end of *modernismo,* and many have looked at it as an attack on *modernismo* in general and even on Rubén Darío in particular. Essentially, the poet is seeking the deeper communication, identifying the swan with shallow beauty. Pedro Salinas, the Spanish poet, has pointed out that EGM wanted to wring the swan's neck for much the same reason that Verlaine wanted to wring the neck of eloquence in a slightly different literary context.[2] González Martínez himself, as we have already seen, made a clear distinction between the elegant word and the profound word of *modernismo*.

> Wring the neck of the deceitfully plumed swan
> who sings his white note to the blue of the fountain;
> he only shows off his grace, so does not sense
> the soul of things nor the voice of the landscape.
>
> *(Tuércele el cuello al cisne de engañoso plumaje*
> *que da su nota blanca al azul de la fuente;*
> *él pasea su gracia no más, pero no siente*
> *el alma de las cosas ni la voz del paisaje.)* (I.150)

It is clear that the poet believes that the swan's beauty may deceive us by making us think there is more to beauty than just beauty. The second line of the quatrain, with the use of color imagery that was so common among the *modernistas*, comes very close to satire in this case. It is clear also that the swan achieves none of the communication that EGM finds essential.

It is in the second quatrain that the poet speaks specifically about the act of writing:

> Flee from any form and any language
> that does not accord with the latent rhythm
> of profound life . . .
>
> *(Huye de toda forma y de todo lenguaje*
> *que no vayan acordes con el ritmo latente*
> *de la vida profunda . . .)* (I.150)

We feel here the fidelity of the poetic act. Part of the act is seeking profound communication, and the actual expression of the truth discovered is absolutely dependent on maintaining the act's integrity. The use of the word is, therefore, not simply a question of producing brilliance, but of not betraying any part of the poetic process. Certainly EGM is not condemning *modernista* techniques as techniques. He uses them himself, and in this poem; even if we regard the adjective use in the second line as satirical, there is no question that the "taciturn flight" (*vuelo taciturno*) (I.150) of the owl, in the first tercet, is a typically *modernista* use of the "essential adjective." Since it is not an adjective normally associated with flight, it completely controls the meaning of the noun and, indeed, it would be a more logical modifier for the owl than for the flight. There are other *modernista* effects in the poem, including mythological reference, but it is doubtful that any could be more convincing than the foregoing.

The owl is the symbol that EGM substitutes for the swan, confessing that it may not have the swan's beauty, but will have greater insight, specifically into "the mysterious book of nocturnal silence" (*el misterioso libro del silencio nocturno*). (I.150) The two adjectives are of consummate importance here because they indicate the difficulty of the searching that we must undertake in order to achieve the desired communication. The symbol of the owl is important since EGM became identified with the symbol, and it was the source of the title of his first volume of autobiography.

Several poems of *Hidden Paths* are in the nature of commentaries on the profound search; or perhaps better said, they are poems in which the poet views himself within the search. In general, their tone is optimistic, expectant. They are more similar to the easy philosophies of Amado Nervo than to the careful creation of the moment that is characteristic of EGM. His optimism is more convincing when its roots are in the opposite of effervescent joy, as in "Grief, if by Chance" ("Dolor, si por acaso") and "An Old Sadness" ("Una vieja tristeza"). The latter, by means of a clear contrast, shows the security that is the source of optimism, but its couplets make the form of the poem less than ideal for the contemplative mood. "Grief, if by Chance" proceeds with more dignity and is, to a considerable extent, an amplification of one of the suggestions of "Psalle et sille." Grief comes to the poet, visits, and will obviously come again. The visit is not an unwelcome one, and the very naturalness of it has the creative effect of guiding the poet toward "the infinite clarity of life" (*la infinita claridad de la vida*). (I.115)

"Soul on the Mountain" ("El alma en la montaña") is a remarkable poem of ascending in which the poet invites his soul to accompany him, and even carries on a conversation between poet and soul. It would appear that the anecdotal character of this contrived situation would make the poem highly artificial, but the detail and depth of the poet's expectation—and of ours, because we are with him—make the poem a reassuring, if not entirely satisfying, experience. The heights are attained by poet and soul, and we feel the reality of a more complete life. The poet, pointing this out to his soul, finds the soul in agreement; but when the poet proposes that the two of them live on the mountain, the soul does not respond.

Although the poet knows perfectly well what he can expect from the human muddle, he knows that he cannot detach himself from it definitively, as we have seen in "Pity." It is not always clear what the degree of his commitment is, but we often feel, when he speaks of reunion, that somehow it must incorporate his commitment—or perhaps the integral life that he dreams of will eliminate the human blindness that inhibits the poet. Certainly his utopian vision in "Doux pays" gives us a wonderful feeling of serenity and primitive freshness, a feeling that we can begin it all over again. This is a world in which all is joined, through the suggested grace of Apollo, god of poetry and of healing.

> A divine partnership between human life
> and the life of the world . . . The Apollinian fusion
> of the line's prodigious simplicity
> with the gigantic effort of distant vision.

> (Un divino consorcio entre la vida humana
> y la vida del mundo . . . La fusión apolínea
> entre la prodigiosa sencillez de la línea
> y el esfuerzo gigante de la visión lejana.) (I.122)

II The Death of the Swan

Between the publication of *The Hidden Paths*, 1911, and the publication of *The Death of the Swan* (*La muerte del cisne*), 1915, the changes in EGM's personal circumstances were dramatic. The Revolution had broken out in 1911 and the country was to spend a number of years going through a radical revision. EGM had come to Mexico City that same year. Several years earlier he had spent a few months there, but decided to return to Sinaloa. Now he was definitively in the center of Mexican cultural life. He became an editorial writer for a newspaper opposed to the Revolution. He later regretted having taken this political position, but like many other men of his generation, he did not readily comprehend the Revolution's significance. Under a counter-revolutionary government he filled two political

positions. His father died (his mother had died in 1904). He
became a member of the Atheneum of Youth, a group of intell-
ectuals several years younger than he. He was elected to regular
membership in the Mexican Academy. Although our purpose
is not to fashion from EGM's poetry a peephole into the private
life of the man, some knowledge of his rapidly changing circumstances may enhance our participation in his poetic process.
There can be no doubt that the violent and sometimes contradictory action of the world in which the poet was living would
incline anyone to take account of himself.

The profound search continued, by means of hypersensitive
communication and also through the act of *being* something other
than himself.

> I have already felt myself be a drop
> in some hidden spring;
> in the throat of a bird I have been the song
> and even perfume in the roses' breath.

> (*Ya me he sentido ser la gota
> de algún oculto manantial;
> en la garganta de algún ave he sido nota
> y hasta perfume en los efluvios del rosal.*) (I.166)

These lines from "The Song of Life" ("La canción de la vida")
are actually the third stage in the development of the poem. It
opens with a call from life, and the feeling of the summons
is carried by reference to springtime and to bees. The next four
quatrains are life's description of what we may expect. They
are the second stage of the development and they contain an
idea not noticed earlier in EGM's poetry: that there is not a
soul in every bee, but there is a collective soul for the hive. This
concept is expressed a second time in terms of ants. One hesitates
to say, from an objective standpoint, what philosophical position
this idea represents, if any; from the standpoint of the reader
within the poem, it communicates a sense of belonging in which
there is no conflict between individuals, but it also produces a
feeling of reluctance by means of the suggestion of an amorphous
whole.

The second stage of development is separated from the third
by a repetition of the first stanza. After that, the speaker is the
poet rather than life. His response, in two quatrains, culminates
in the feeling of reunion quoted above. In the final stage, the
last quatrain, the poet explains that deep within him, his own

soul maintains its particularity. Our uncertainty is quieted, because the feeling here is that we can be a part of creation without losing identity.

The sense of being all things is expanded and deepened in "Flickering Spirit" ("Anima trémula"), a poem that contains perhaps the most yearning of any of EGM's work. The intensity of the feeling is similar to that developed in his best sonnets, but the trajectory of this particular poem requires a fuller statement. It is written in stanzas of irregular lengths, amounting to sixty lines in all. The reader's response is likely to be good because the poet pulls him into his own vortex of sensitivity, but it is a difficult and tiring experience. The first line is "There is a gentle sorrow in my hope" (*Hay un suave dolor en mi esperanza*), (I.168) but this sorrow does not overcome the desire to ascend. Then, addressing the soul, EGM changes to the past tense and speaks of what the soul has dreamed. Often the poet uses the past tense at great risk; that is, frequently it makes him talk about the resplendent moment rather than create it. But in this poem, the strength of the persistent expectation, even in spite of sorrow, carries on throughout the whole poem. In a remarkable series of images—some familiar and some new—the poet creates more than a feeling of uniting with specific things. Here the sense of integration becomes cosmic in two ways: by extending the metaphor to include the farthest reaches of the universe, and by a contrasting minuteness of the special quality of our own being.

> To be the lamp of love in the distant
> explosion of a star whose light
> may never arrive and who is sister
> of the sun's fire that strikes the peak.

> (*Ser lámpara de amor en la lejana*
> *combustíon de una estrella cuya lumbre*
> *nunca habrá de llegar, y que es hermana*
> *de la flama del sol que da en la cumbre.*) (I.169)

This grandiose and wonderful expectation is complemented in the following stanza by another that concentrates on the individual being, but makes that being, within itself, a wholeness that consists of both ends of the act:

> and to be equally viewer and spectacle,
> and to be the dreamer, and to be the dream.

> *(y ser, al par, vidente y espectáculo,*
> *y ser el soñador, y ser el sueño.)* (I.170)

In still another direction, the poem enlarges expectation through the feeling that "death is one of the many rhythms of life" (*la muerte es un ritmo de tantos de la vida*). (I.170) The last stanza makes a circle by indirect reference to the first stanza. The feeling of yearning is intensified to the point of sorrow or of pain (*dolor* means both) and still we know that both desire and search will continue.

The poet's sorrow, pain, or anguish (the most appropriate English interpretation depends on the general feeling of a particular poem) comes either because the resplendent moment is elusive or because—to repeat what we have already observed —we can expect a revelation beyond that moment, or at least pursue it interminably. In spite of his anguish, EGM recalls one moment in "To a Stone in the Road" ("A una piedra del camino"). He frames the memory between two statements of the same stanza, one that expresses gratitude for the moment. Then, using the same framing technique in "To an Ingenuous Soul" ("A un alma ingenua"), the poet wishes for the state of innocence that would allow him to be close to things. The reader is likely to respect the poet in these two pieces, but he is not incorporated into the poetic process, because there is no development, the poems do not exert the influence of emotional movement. We understand that innocence is desirable for the communication that we seek, just as silence is, but the feeling of innocence is not in the poem. It is mentioned, but not sensed.

We have a feeling of looking at the poetic quest rather than participating in it. It is as if we were somehow detached from ourselves, asking what it is all about. "The Useless Days" ("Los días inútiles") combines past and present in our awareness with a sudden, rushing recall of all that has happened. And the poet says, in some astonishment and considerable disappointment, "But I am the same, I am the same as yesterday" (*Pero yo soy el mismo, soy el mismo de ayer*). (I.175) The source of anguish in this poem is less the regret for past acts than disillusionment for not having been essentially changed by all that has happened. "Stanzas" ("Estancias") is to a considerable extent an amplification of "The Useless Days." Perhaps they are more like a variation on the theme, since they add more feeling than insight. Four of the six quatrains are questions, only questions—

a rare phenomenon in EGM's poetry up to this time, and obviously the voice of a man who has become acutely aware of
the passing of his own days. He asks, in successive stanzas,
what will become of his eyes, hands, mouth, ears. These have
been the instruments of the search which, according to the fifth
stanza, has been unproductive. And in the last, he faces life's
horrifying question, "What have you done?" (*qué has hecho?*)
(I.177)

Returning to the sonnet, EGM finds the remedy for anguish
in "My Friend Silence" ("Mi amigo el silencio"). It is important
that the word (name) "silence" is mentioned only in the title
of the poem. Within the poem itself, the author simply assumes
the validity of silence as a person. Silence soothes his discontent,
and in the sextet:

> We go along the fleeting pathways,
> and our quiet travellers' step
> does not wake the birds . . . We go
>   alone through the unfamiliar region;
> and in the vast quiet, only life
> comes out to hear the verse we do not say.
>
> (*Vamos por el huir de los senderos,*
> *y nuestro mudo paso de viajeros*
> *no despierta a los pájaros . . . Pasamos*
>   *solos por la región desconocida;*
> *y en la vasta quietud, no más la vida*
> *sale a escuchar el verso que callamos.*) (I.183)

"Hortus conclusus" is another very fine sonnet that communicates the poet's turning inward. Past and future combine here
and he is aware both of souls that were and of souls that are
yet to be. His own soul does not respond to their seeking
entrance. But these two sonnets contain within themselves a
strange contradiction. Unlike the poems where the poet is seen
from the outside, both author and reader are in creative movement in these sonnets. In the very act of retiring from the quest,
we participate in it, with every line contributing to our comprehension of what is real.

In a very long poem, "The Song" ("La Canción"), EGM
captures the feeling of the everlastingness of the ultimate truth.
Referring to his own song, he expresses his reaching out to all
things animate and inanimate; then he extends the quest spa-
tially, adding substantially to the feeling through images that

suggest vagueness, illusion—a mirage effect. Then his song reaches out to humanity. But at the end of each of these sections, he refers to *the* song, which is different from his own; and this larger song is more authentic for being withdrawn into the soul. And finally, when all creation rolls into the abyss, when everything that exists is lost, *the* song continues, ineffably intense. Here again, while reaching out on one level seems to fail, we are aware of the persistence of an ultimate goal. Certainly it is the mission of the poet—of all poets—to hear the song.

The persistence of the poets themselves is felt keenly in "Tomorrow the Poets" ("Mañana los poetas"). This is a sonnet with an interesting effect of alternating—we might even say flickering—pessimism and optimism. The first quatrain predicts that tomorrow's poets will sing what is impossible for the poets of today; in the second, they will laugh at the old-fashioned striving. In the first tercet, they will run into the same impossibility; and in the second, they will sing exactly the same song. There is, of course, a feeling of futility here, and it is reinforced by expressions like "useless," "in vain," "darkness," and the image of the abandoned lyre in the dust. But this feeling is counterbalanced by "new constellations," "another destiny," and particularly by "restless souls." While the optimistic weight of the poem is near the beginning, we retain the impression of the restless souls which characterize the poets of whatever time, and the impression is particularly rewarding when we recall it at the end, as tomorrow's poets sing the same song. We feel then that what is important is not the answer to the ultimate question, but the persistence of the search.

III The Book of Strength, Goodness, and Dream

This volume of unwieldy title in English or in Spanish (*El libro de la fuerza, de la bondad y del ensueño*) continues along many of the lines followed in *The Death of the Swan.* Published in 1917, it reveals a tendency toward longer poems with considerable variety in line length. Stanza length often varies within the poem. The sonnet all but disappears. EGM experiments with tercets and with counterpointing sets of couplets that form a quatrain. He also uses a series of long lines with couplet rhyming but not divided into stanzas; the effect is almost as close to rhythmic prose as it is to poetry. Generally speaking, these differences in form are noticed after the reading rather than earlier. The greater length of the individual poem is the only change that is immediately impressive. With few exceptions the form is suitable for what the poet wants to do, and as is almost always the case in EGM's poetry, form is unobtrusive. The thematic lines are the concern for seeing reality, the limits of knowing, and the unresponsiveness of the worldly crowd.

The poet's anxiety over human insensitivity urges him to prophetic statement in "Sacred Wind" ("Viento sagrado"), a foreshadowing of *The Flood of Fire* (*El diluvio de fuego*) and other poems of disaster that were written more than twenty years later. In a series of tercets "Sacred Wind" sweeps the earth, bringing a new era with it. It will be an era of justice and brotherhood, and it will also be a time of intensity of life, of increased awareness. The predictions of the wind's actions continue for about two-thirds of the poem, and culminate in the union of earth and heaven. The poem then describes the utopian result, which is a state of complete communion among animals, things, and men. The trouble with this poem is that the author talks about communion, but we don't really feel it. What we do feel is anxiety—the anxiety of wishful thinking. The last tercet is written in a "woe unto him" tone, and implies dire circumstances for those who close their ears to the voice and for those who hear but do not heed.

The fate of the unheeding becomes abundantly clear in "Dead Souls" ("Las almas muertas") which is wonderfully creative because EGM reinforces his imagery very skillfully. The first stanza sets a scene that is completely somber. "Gray mist" and "foreboding light" are overwhelming along "the sinister routes of evil" (*las siniestras rutas del mal*); and on this dreary journey, the poet reinforces sight with sound as we hear "a crunching of branches" and "a flying of dry leaves." (I.222) Subsequent stanzas maintain the lugubrious atmosphere and communicate the feeling of human foolishness and carelessness, then the completely insensitive herd, and finally, the utter impossibility of changing the situation. The poet's only hope is within his own soul whose sensitivity separates him—and us—from the general desolation.

In this volume perhaps more than in any other, EGM insists on the need to ascend. Even such a poignant song as "The Girl Who Has not Seen the Sea" ("La muchacha que no ha visto el mar") suggests the need of reaching out, of moving beyond the limits of constricting experience to discover what we have never even dreamed. In "The Prayer of the Sterile Rock" ("La plegaria de la roca estéril"), we experience a kind of reverse development which reduces communion to its barest essential. The rock is isolated, barren, in communion with nothing. It has neither stream nor moss; it is only rock, and yearning. Five quatrains of reduction lead to the prayer of the sixth, that an eagle build its nest on the rock. Then in the seventh, there is a beautiful addendum of creative resignation: that, if even this desperate chance for communion be impossible, the rock become a symbol of the most elevated solitude. The personification of the rock (it speaks in the first person) is slightly disconcerting at the beginning, but the feeling rapidly becomes our own.

A particularly brilliant sense of reunion, of concentration within a given moment, comes alive in "Strange Bondage" ("Extraña sujeción"), where the union of things and beings is reinforced by the unity of time and of the emotions that are placed along time's supposed trajectory. The first stanza is really a preface in which the poet sets the stage for the development that will come later.

> A strange bondage ties my life
> to the fleeting moment. Why do I not lose
> the thread of things . . .
>
> (*Extraña sujeción ata mi vida*
> *al momento fugaz. ¿Por qué no pierdo*
> *el hilo de las cosas . . .*) (I.273)

In many poems of this volume and the one preceding, EGM speaks of the past: of attitudes cast aside, of opportunities lost, of memories that bring pain. In "The Useless Days" he is disturbed by the realization that he is still the same person. Here it is continuity that puzzles him, and it is more than simple recall of things that have happened. The memory, in the second stanza, is "bedazzling" (*alucinante*) (I.273) and is related to the present circumstance. We have a feeling of *déjà vu* when the poet says

> I have heard before that voice and that sigh,
> and every face is an evocation.
>
> (*ya he escuchado esa voz y ese suspiro,*
> *y es una evocación cada semblante.*) (I.273)

He brings the feeling of unity to an early climax in the third
stanza, stating the fact as clearly as he can in the rational terms
of the first two lines, and creating a reverberating continuity
with the strange echoes of the last two. Here is the minute
universe:

> Everything is within me; neither time nor distance
> succeeds in erasing the deep imprint;
> there is an echo of light in every star
> and in every flower an echo of fragrance.

> (*Todo está en mí; ni tiempo ni distancia*
> *borrar consiguen la profunda huella;*
> *hay un eco de luz en cada estrella*
> *y en cada flor un eco de fragancia.*) (I.273)

The next stanza concentrates the sense of the omnitemporal
present and the gigantic significance of the moment. In the
two following stanzas, the poet makes a relationship between
his past acts, both good and bad, and his communication with
things. The now familiar imagery is very effective in representing
a unified creation in which time, also unified, may be a part.
The seventh stanza then reiterates the unity of time by creating
a feeling of the reality of the past within what has not yet
happened. The eighth stanza supports the seventh with examples, and the last is a beautiful burst of lyric uncertainty that
carries the positive quality of sensing accurately what we cannot
know or say in any other terms.

> In my dazzlement truth is
> confused with shadows, and I think
> that long ago I dreamed what now I see
> or I am dreaming of my life itself.

> (*En mi alucinación va confundida*
> *la verdad con las sombras, y yo creo*
> *que ha mucho que soñé lo que a hora veo*
> *o estoy soñando con mi propia vida.*) (I.274)

It is clear here that the poet is not giving up the quest, whatever his doubts may be, just as it is clear in "The Only Verse"
("El único verso") that he is aware of the significance of the
moment: "grasp the instant in flight in order to make it live"
(*coge el instante al vuelo para hacerlo vivir*). (I.272) What
bothers him most is the tragedy of the limits of knowing. But
the quest continues, and at his best, EGM takes us into the

moment when we face the limits of knowing and find a certain reconciliation by taking the search to the farthest point. "The Sphinx" ("La esfinge") uses the title symbol for the unavailability of ultimate knowing, but this beautiful poem is really a use of the beloved as a means of reaching the farthest limits of communion, of reunion.

At the beginning of the poem, the author uses "while" to introduce two statements of the circumstance in which the beloved and the poet find themselves. The introductory word itself gives us a sharp feeling of actuality that is strengthened immediately by the motion of "we go" or "we pass" (*vamos*). From the beginning there is a sense of the unity of the two because "our shadows are melded into one" (*confundidas nuestras sombras en una*). (I.252) The feeling of the statement following the first "while" is one of gentle sorrow and of tremendous security in the awareness of belonging to each other. The second "while" statement establishes the identity of beloved and poet, and carries a sense of the similarity between her reaching out in love and his reaching out in poetry. Then, given this realization of their relationship, we know that they face each other, each one seeking the eternal truth in the other. The poet knows that they have done this many times before, and the sphinx has not answered. Then, in an interlude of six lines, we sense the poet before the mystery of the human soul, dismayed by the inability of one soul to know another.

In the latter half of the poem, we identify completely with the lovers' attempt to comprehend each other. We know that although they are in some sense united, the joining is incomplete because they cannot reveal themselves fully to each other.

> I, like you, try to attach myself to life
> with a limitless love; to penetrate the secret
> heart of beings; to break down the obstacle
> that hides from our eyes the divine spectacle
> of august truth . . . And it is a futile insistence;

> (*Yo, como tú, pretendo allegarme a la vida*
> *con un amor sin límites; penetrar la escondida*
> *entraña de los seres; quebrantar el obstáculo*
> *que oculta a nuestros ojos el divino espectáculo*
> *de la verdad augusta . . . Y es inútil empeño;*) (I.253)

In the remaining ten lines of the poem, we feel the beauty of this love that inspires the search, that is indeed the instrument of the search. The awareness of the silence of the sphinx does not lessen the exaltation of the quest. And although we have a certain feeling of cosmic tragedy, there is a tentative fulfillment in the degree of union achieved.

Your eyes that kiss me and your voice that calls my name
will never be able to offer me more than the vain shadow
of a soul that you yourself do not know; and one day
you will discover that I am not yours and you cannot be mine.
After impossible longing, our errant souls
will see each other from afar like two travellers.
In their eternal wavering, the souls of men
play hide-and-seek; and life permits
only that the moon, in its secret pity,
make of our souls a single silhouette.

(Tus ojos que me besan y tu voz que me nombra
no podrán ofrecerme sino la vana sombra
de un alma que tú misma desconoces; y un día
sabrás que no soy tuyo ni tú puedes ser mía.
Tras anhelo imposible, nuestras almas errantes
se verán desde lejos como dos caminantes.
En su vaivén eterno, juegan al escondite
las almas de los hombres; y la vida permite
apenas que la luna, en su piedad secreta,
haga de nuestras almas una sola silueta.) (I.253)

What we feel here is not the end of love, but the limit of worldly knowing. There is no desperation, only an intense yearning.

"Meditation Under the Moon" ("Meditación bajo la luna") is a poem of solitude, solitude consciously sought by the poet so he can contemplate his own state. The series of thirty-one stanzas is divided into three more or less equal parts. The linked tercets (the blank ending of the middle line of one tercet becomes the rhyme of the next) add to the continuity of the impression. The last stanza of each of the three sections has an extra line which makes it a quatrain in a-b-a-b rhyme. The additional line provides an appropriate terminal effect in each section.

The poet makes no assumptions and is careful to build the atmosphere of the garden where his meditation takes place. The feeling is of silence, serenity, shadow—words and concepts that are incorporated into his imagery. And within this gratifying isolation, there is the promise of something beyond the commonplace: it is "a night of mysterious opalescences" (*una noche de opalescencias misteriosas*). (I.255) After establishing the setting, the poet begins to dream, and his dreaming turns out to be as much experience as imagination, because it is a combination of intellect and emotion that reveals the poet's state. The dreaming has an unusual quality that EGM compares to the dreaming of his youth, when his soul was "purer, more ingenuous, and less mine" (*más pura, más ingenua y menos mía*).(I.255) We sense here, though the poet does not develop it, the eternal problem of the ego. The fact that his soul, when it was in a purer state, was less his own suggests that the process of living has brought about a kind of contamination that is opposed to the purity needed for the most profound communication. To put it another way, the growth of worldly identity progressively alienates us from primordial union, and so our soul is more than our own. However, within the poem these considerations flash past, and the feeling of the rest of the first section emanates from the fear of having to relive the past constantly. Here the poet's awareness that he may indeed be just the same as always takes on a haunting quality.

The second section is a process of proving, by reference to his poetry, that he is different, that change has taken place. Since his reaction to the "old song" (*antigua canción*) is different, he must not be the same. At the end of this section, as at the end of the first, the poet asks for serenity. The third section is the history of his ascent. EGM uses the past tense to describe the act of ascending, solitary and climbing. The inspiration that supports his struggle is a voice whose promise is that "at last the mirage will disappear" (*el espejismo desaparece al fin*). (I.258) In the following tercet, we have the sudden feeling of revelation. Everything looks different, light replaces darkness; and the light is the poet's own being. But EGM is not going to rest on false hopes in this poem. In the two tercets immediately following the revelation, we feel anguish and the uncertainty of not knowing just what the destination is. The feeling is communicated specifically by a question that the poet shouts within the poem itself. It has the effect of breaking the comfortable spell of the revelation, and we—along with the poet—are overcome by loneliness. What remains is silence. The ascent ends in a tower of silence. We know that the very worst we can be is a human interpretation of the sterile rock—a perfect solitude. Having reached this point, the serenity asked for at the ends of the first two sections now is granted, and it cannot be disturbed by exterior confusion.

IV Parables and Other Poems

Throughout the poetry of Gónzalez Martínez there is a hint of didacticism. Generally speaking, it is well controlled; however, his growing concern over the difficulty of resolving problems, of finding the ultimate answer, and of expressing even what he was able to discover, probably caused him to undertake the moral teaching of *Parábolas* (*Parables*), 1918. The lessons are admirable and probably contribute to the author's exemplary moral influence, but as poetry the parables are among his least successful work. The reason is that there is no particular point in expressing a moral in verse unless verse can make the understanding clearer or deeper than prose can. Not all the poems called parables are parables in fact. And those that are not really parables tend to be better poetry than those that are, because the author's poetic development is freer when he is not restricted by a predetermined goal.

The "Parable of the Nameless Guest" ("Parábola del huésped sin nombre") has two notably high points. After the unknown guest has entered the poet's house, the latter asks his name. The guest replies that he knows nothing of himself, not even his name, but asks the poet if it is not enough that he is a man. The question creates in the poet a moment of unusual awareness of himself.

> At his words I think that my life
> is a suspended question
> in the silent mystery . . .
>
> (*A sus palabras pienso que mi vida*
> *es como una pregunta suspendida*
> *en el arcana mudo* . . .) (II.4)

Then, when the guest is inside and the two are silent in the presence of each other, their shadows are projected, elongated, reaching out in a way that ordinary prose would hardly communicate.

In "Parable of the Brother" (Parábola del hermano") we find an interesting statement of the nature of the poet's commitment to men. He says that his brother is

the one who shares my anguish and goes with me
along the same road, not the beggar
who holds out his hand to me.

(el que tiene mi angustia y va conmigo
por idéntica ruta, no el mendigo
que me tiende la mano.) (II.17)

Indeed he will give the beggar what matters least, but what he really gives of himself goes to his brother. The awareness of this relationship is something of an antidote to the feeling of frustration that we get from "Parable of the Useless Task" ("Parábola de la tarea inútil"). In this parable, the poet talks with a child who says he is emptying the sea and relates the task to his own endless striving. A feeling of the limits of knowing emanates from "Parable of the Door" (Parábola de la puerta") where we (the poem uses the first person plural) try to gain entrance and, after the long struggle, enter and find the mansion empty.

Luisa Luisi suggests that the enigmatic "we" of this poem are EGM and Amado Nervo.[3] In his later years, Nervo found serenity in Christian faith, and according to Luisi, this poem could be part of a discussion between the two writers, with EGM expressing his doubt here. This is not to suggest that he was an irreligious man, but that he would not settle for an easy answer. It seems that EGM's poetry is in itself the answer; that is, the answer is in the search, or in the vertical movement, or in the tragic anguish of not finding the answer. It is unlikely that the empty mansion of this poem represents, as Luisi suggests, a disbelief in an after-life; rather, it is an expression of necessary doubt, the obverse of the certainty we often feel with regard to discovering the secret. Out of the synthesis of the two, EGM gains access to some degree of profound communication. The expectation of communion is quite apparent in "Parable of the Sea, the Wind, and the Moon" ("Parábola del mar, del viento, y de la luna"). This poem is not a parable at all, but the creation of three resplendent moments when communion is established because we not only enter the sea, the wind, and the moon, they enter us. Although the moments are described and related as if they happened to an old man, the device is unimportant. The moments belong to the poet because he makes them within the poem, and gives them to us.

EGM's poetic search has by this time reached the point of painful honesty. This quality, sufficiently apparent in earlier volumes, is concentrated here. Sometimes there is great confidence, sometimes great anguish, very often an obvious groping among the possibilities of understanding. The poems that follow the thirteen parables involve us in the beautiful courage of the poet's persistent search.

"Like a Crystal Sigh" ("Como un suspiro de cristal") is a yearning for purity. It is a combination of thinking and feeling, and the unusual rhyming contributes greatly to the combination. The poem is written in eight quatrains, and in each of these stanzas complete rhyme occurs at the end of the first line, the middle of the second, and the end of the third; assonance occurs at the end of the second and the end of the fourth. (Since the point of the following example is to show the rhyme, the Spanish version is given first.)

> *Al borde llego de la fuente*
> *— ¡qué mansamente el agua va! —*
> *y oigo el rumor de la corriente*
> *como un suspiro de cristal.*
>
> (I come to the edge of the spring
> — how gently the water flows! —
> and I hear the murmur of the current
> as if it were a crystal sigh.) (II.40)

The effect of this scheme through eight stanzas is understandably greater than a single stanza can indicate. The mid-line rhyme of the second line comes so quickly after the first rhyming that we are caught, as if a thought were interrupted and almost dropped. But then the rest of the second line comes as if it were more purposeful, and we are more aware of what the second part of the line says. It is, therefore, very strongly accented in our impression as compared to the preceding line and a half. Furthermore, it sets us in a contemplative mood for the last two lines which use appropriate images to express the poet's feeling. The contrasting smoothness of the last two lines—contrasting, that is, with the interruption in the first two—captures the feeling of the flowing of water, the leitmotif of the poem. But both rhymes, the full rhyme and the assonantal, tie the two sets of lines to each other, so there is no abrupt shift within the stanza. Thought and sensory response are very effectively linked.

We become aware, in the second stanza, of a feeling of doubt which is related to the vanishing day (accented by its position at the end of the second line). Then comes the yearning to be good as in a time now past. Here again is the feeling of "Meditation Under the Moon"; the time past refers to a purer state when our soul was less our own. In the two following stanzas, the water imagery is direct, and the poet wishes to be water so he could have its purity. The wishing to be water impresses us here in a different way from the desire to be things in other poems. Here we have not so much the feeling of reunion as a sense of the need to change. The desire to be water is the need to be something different from what we are.

Rather than multiply the statement of the second and fourth stanzas, EGM, in the fifth stanza, brings us into the world where the water is, by hearing a distant bell and a bird's song. Having placed us fully within the world of nature, he then picks a flower which is related to the water by the drop of dew that trembles on it. And in the seventh stanza he pulls off the petals and drops them on the flowing water. At the end of this stanza he makes another reference to the vanishing day, relating the last part of the poem to the earlier part, and also relating the disappearing day to the flowing water. The eighth stanza is very similar to the first, though not a copy of it, and we end with the original emotion augmented by the experience within the frame. Although a great deal has happened between the first and last verses in terms of meditation and emotional experience, the containment of our reaction within the frame has increased the yearning.

We find a change in the desire for communication in "New Soul" ("Alma nueva"), where the poet has renounced the quest for knowing. He announces his new attitude in the first line: "Now I have curbed my longing to know it all" (*Ya refrené mis ansias de conocerlo todo*). (II.44) What he prefers now is an aimless wandering, but not simply the comfortable way, since he goes "with my face to the biting wind and my feet in the mud" (*con la frente a los cierzos y los pies en el lodo*). (II:44) He develops his feeling by saying that he wants "to feel everything like a vast heart in the middle of the universe." (II.44) Obviously, he is not choosing an easier way, but seeking a possible way. The change is described in terms of a transition from rational knowing to feeling; the poet wants to be all emotion, "Like roses that tremble for everything, and know nothing" (*Como las rosas que a todo tiemblan, y que nada saben*). (II.44) The problem for EGM's reader, at this point, is that the knowing we have anticipated with the poet has never been knowledge that could be expressed in rational terms, so we must sense the difference between the aggressive search for the light that would reveal the deepest truth, and a cultivated openness that is receptive to any emotion that is alive in the universe.

The poet finds, in "The Impossible Return" ("El retorno imposible"), that trying to recover the past is pointless, yet he feels unavoidably linked to it, just as he felt in "Strange Bondage." Here the trip is a dream, and although the poet informs us from the beginning that it will not take place, the dream itself takes on importance because the nature of the trip is serious. The memory of the past evokes a certain amount of gaiety because the spring is "tuneful and merry" (*cantarina y jocunda*). (II.42) Association of the spring here with the spring of "Like a Crystal Sigh," combines purity and joy. But this brief festival burst in the poem belongs to the past, and contrasts with the seriousness that would characterize the journey if it were undertaken. At the beginning of the poem we feel a mixture of yearning to relive the past and relief that it does not have to be relived.

The first element of the mixed emotion, the yearning, is developed in four couplets that recall opportunities for communication that have been lost. The four stanzas refer to four kinds of things: animal (bird), vegetal (tree), inanimate (stone), cosmic (sun). Through these four verses, EGM reconstructs the universe with which he has sought communion, expanding it from the most probable response outward to include all. Then in a quatrain he confesses the lost opportunities.

The poem continues in three irregular stanzas of diminishing length. The first is a voice that invites the poet to relive the past—perhaps it is more temptation than invitation. The next stanza develops the second facet of the mixed emotion, that is, relief that the past does not have to be relived. The manner of expression is a question in which we feel the assurance that even better opportunities lie ahead. But even in the midst of this forward thrust, we look back, in the last stanza, not knowing why, but caught "between what I remember and what I foresee" (*entre lo que recuerdo y lo que adivino*). (II.43) So the author dreams of the trip that he will never take.

The insistent past is seen also in "Autumn Song" ("Canción de otoño"), where memory coincides with the natural setting, but later remains constant even though nature changes. The memory comes with rain that is pleasant and painful at the same time; and so is the memory, for "my soul and the afternoon were sobbing together" (*mi alma y la tarde sollozaban al par*). (II.48) In the next to the last stanza, the rain disappears and nature becomes a contrast to the mood of the poem. But in the final stanza, the memory persists.

"Afternoons of Those Years" ("Tardes de aquellos años") is an autobiographical meditation in which we view four stages of the poet's life, in four stanzas. The first is a time when the poet is aware only of the present, where the past has no meaning and the future is full of promises. Life is trivial, and it is like the dust of a road in which footprints are erased and forgotten by those who come later. Life becomes a song in the second stanza, and we feel joy and expectation. The third stanza is the time of the writing of this book—a time of awareness of the past, of longing, of sorrow. Rather than a song, life is now a book; and in spite of the fact that much of the book is disillusionment, it contains something of the poet's reaching out, and he always carries it with him, along with "the fever of my vain desire" (*la fiebre de mi vano deseo*). (II.62) The prospect for the future, in the fourth stanza, is something less than exciting. The feeling is more than calm, it is passive. The silence that the poet mentions in the last stanza is not the promised solitude of the heights, but the "deep silence of an empty house" (*hondo silencio de una casa vacía*). (II.62)

This note of pessimism is not really surprising in the context of uncertainty that characterizes this volume of poems. However, there are other poems that are optimistic and are more in accord with EGM's active searching in one direction or another, however strong his uncertainty may be. "Reredos" ("Retablo") is an exhortation to remember precisely this active nature of life. And it is well to recall that very often when EGM uses the second person address or imperative, he appears to be speaking to himself. When he says, in the first line of "Reredos," "Make of your life a mystic reredos of hopes" (*Haz de tu vida un místico retablo de esperanzas*), (II.53) he is projecting into

the future with a sense of continuity that is anything but passive.
The word "esperanzas" might very well be given in English as
"expectation" in this context. Using this reredos as the scene
against which life goes on in a process that is a kind of worship,
we reach the point of feeling that emotion is more than physical
life, and will endure.

The feeling of endurance is magnificently created through the
imagery of the persistent heart in one of EGM's best poems,
"Incessant Heart" ("Corazón incesante"). And the beating continues in circumstances far different from sunny enthusiasm.

> I have attended the mysterious twilight that extinguishes
> harmonious landscapes and colored skies,
> and whose cold hand quiets the sounds
> of birds that tremble beneath the malevolent shadow.

> (He asistido al misterio crepuscular que apaga
> campiñas armoniosas y cielos de colores,
> y que con mano gélida va acallando rumores
> de pájaros que tiemblan bajo la sombra aciaga.) (II.49)

Here is the background for pessimism. The stanza suggests
darkness, coldness, lifelessness. The feeling continues through
the first part of the next stanza, but at its end, hope suggests
the active role.

> That night immobile in its lethal repose,
> reigns over the antrums where my dreams sleep,
> and makes tears fall; but the divine seed
> of hope drinks my silent weeping.

> (Aquella noche inmóvil en su letal reposo,
> reina sobre los antros en que mis sueños duermen
> y hace caer mis lágrimas; pero el divino germen
> de la esperanza bebe mi llanto silencioso.) (II.49)

Here hope is clearly in ascendancy over disillusionment. And
it is not just a statement of fact, but the creation of the feeling
within the poem. EGM accomplishes the miracle by not denying
the existence of sorrow, rather he sustains its thread. But at the
same time, the undying hope becomes more and more powerful.
In the third stanza, the "poet heart" (corazón poeta) keeps
singing even in the presence of death-like disillusionment. In
the fourth, the poet has sometimes thought that the heart's
persistence is simply torture. Life obviously goes on, the search
continues. Then in the final stanza, the persistence of the emotion
is triumphant.

The great silence vainly marks the sun's
leaving, and the earth like an inert mass
goes rolling in the abyss . . . Triumphant over death,
you beat, poor heart, tolling life.

*(En vano el gran silencio comenta la partida
del sol, y va la tierra como una masa inerte
rodando en los abisimos . . . Triunfador de la muerte,
tú lates, pobre entraña, repicando a la vida.)* (II.50)

CHAPTER 3

The Astonishing World

> Where is life that I may
> crush it in my arms? —
> "The Tragic Hour"

I   Word of the Wind

BY the early 1920's, Mexico had many characteristics of a nation in the process of reshaping itself. The military phase of the Revolution was over, and the people were beginning to work their way out of the shock that the long series of rebellions had caused. The road into the future called for a great deal of stock-taking and of debating about the nature and destiny of the country. The need of renewal affected the arts as well as other aspects of the culture. These were the years of Diego Rivera and Carlos Chávez, and they were also the youthful years of the poets most closely associated with the vanguardist trends of the time.

In the preceding decade, the brilliant poetic voices of Mexico were Ramón López Velarde and Enrique González Martínez. Each followed a path that was peculiarly his own. López Velarde extracted the essence of his provincial background, and built on it a poetic edifice that incorporated a masterful revelation of his own humanness. As he reached outward in the expression of his anguish, his poetry became quite as universal as EGM's, though by a different process. González Martínez was, without any effort on his part, more universally oriented from the beginning. While López Velarde established his identity by primary reference to what was intimately his own, EGM discovered first the magic of poetry and then proceeded to communicate with the natural—rather than the human—aspect of the universe. López Velarde died when he was still very young, in 1921. He left a strong imprint on Mexican poetry; but it is doubtful that, even had he lived, he would have been the leader

70

that the young poets lacked. González Martínez also was influential, though certainly not in the sense of promoting poetic novelty. In his quiet way, he was more inspiration than leader. Frank Dauster has said that EGM's influence on contemporary Mexican poetry has to be found in attitudes rather than in words.[1]

In 1920, one year before the publication of *Word of the Wind* (*La palabra del viento*), EGM was appointed minister plenipotentiary to Chile. Two years later he went to Argentina in the same capacity, and then to Spain in 1924. He was minister there until his return to Mexico in 1931. Travel affected the poet in two ways. One of its effects was the satisfaction of an old yearning. The act of physically extending horizons, of being carried by the sea, would naturally be important to a writer whose poetic imagination reached out in precisely those terms. The other effect of his ambassadorship is that he met many of the literary people in the countries where he served. These friendships strengthened the universality of his point of view, and they also placed him in contact with vanguardist[2] poetry. He certainly never became a vanguardist poet; but there were changes in his work that probably were motivated by the new directions, and we have some reason to think that for a while he may have felt overwhelmed by them. This influence is seen principally in *Bedazzled Pilgrim* (*El romero alucinado*), published in 1923, and in *Subtle Tokens* (*Las señales furtivas*), in 1925.

Word of the Wind is the sound of the poet's voice at the beginning of his diplomatic career. We continue to be aware of the poet's difficulty with the past, a feeling that motivated him to recapture some of the moments of childhood in a group of poems called "Restless Childhood" ("La niñez inquieta"); and we see the continued contemplation of his human condition in a sonnet series called "Poem of the Seven Sins" ("Poema de los siete pecados"). In the title poem of *Word of the Wind*, EGM creates the resplendent moment of his awareness of himself and of the presentness of time. The experience is developed in a rising line throughout seven quatrains, with foreshadowing in the first, a tentative summation in the fourth which is reinforced in the sixth, and full awareness in the last stanza.

We are prepared to expect greater than usual insight when the first lines announce

> While the breezes prophesied in the foliage
> the verses that the poet someday will sing,
>
> (*Mientras vaticinaban las brisas en la fronda*
> *los versos que el poeta un día ha de cantar,*) (II.77)

Then our expectation is increased immediately when the poet indicates that his emotion is deeper even than his reaction to night or to the sea. The significance of this suggestion by González Martínez looms large for the reader who knows his poetry. The second stanza promises revelation through the use of "augury" and "rare evocation," but particularly by reference to the "hour when the mountain opens its heart" (*hora en que el monte abre su corazón*). (II.77) The fusion of time begins in the third stanza when "the prestige of past illusion was joined/ to the infinite anguish of what is to come" (*se sumaba el prestigio de la ilusión pasada/a la infinita angustia de lo que ha de venir*). (II.77) Here the verbal constructions give a sense of the past followed immediately by a sense of the future, just as in the first two lines of the poem. The effect on the reader is to leave us in an unidentified present, if we do not unite with the poem; but if we do, the present not only becomes identified, but is indeed unique—it is all. The fourth stanza, a tentative summation, communicates both the fusion of time and the evanescent quality of the moment when we are aware of the joining.

> I felt that my awareness was coming from faraway
> centuries, and that tomorrow and yesterday alike
> were clasping hands in the voracious minute
> like night fleeing with the dawn.
>
> (*Sentí que mi conciencia venía de lejanos*
> *siglos, y que el mañana, lo mismo que el ayer,*
> *en el voraz minuto se estrechaban las manos*
> *como la noche en fuga con el amanecer.*) (II.77)

Again in the fifth stanza, the contrasting and combining of past and future produce the acute sense of the present. The sixth stanza reinforces the fourth when "I felt that a thousand centuries were forging my destiny" (*Sentí que mil centurias forjaban mi destino*), (II.78) and then produces a strong will to move forward. The moment is complete in the last stanza:

> And my hand wanted to seize, in the fleeting moment,
> all my anxieties and my future action at the same time,
> and my spirit understood the word of the wind . . .
> And the heart of the mountain beat in my heart!

(Y quiso asir mi mano, en el fugaz momento,
al par mis ansias todas y mi futura acción,
y comprendió mi espíritu la palabra del viento . . .
Y el corazón del monte latió en mi corazón!) (II.77)

This poem is, on one level, the second creation of what has been experienced; but on a different plane, the past sense of the poem becomes not the past of the experience referred to, but the past of life. The moment comes alive in the joining of past and present and very briefly we are, if not the discoverers of ultimate reality, at least a part of all that exists.

In "The New Sense" ("El nuevo sentido"), we feel the terrible monotony of reality repeated; we are lacking the additional sense that would make constant creation. The poet wants more than reunion with what exists; he wants to be the cutting edge of creativity. The poem's basic statement is in the form of a complaint that all that exists is a sad monotony.

To see that the rectifying hours
are, to consciousness, only those same hours
that we saw lost in the abyss of time,
and the heart . . . a perennial plagiarism of itself.

(Ver que las horas rectificadoras
no son a la conciencia sino las mismas horas
que miramos hundirse del tiempo en el abismo,
y el corazón . . . un plagio perenne de sí mismo.) (II.79)

This poetic emotion cannot be fully appreciated unless we maintain the awareness of the fusion of time in "Word of the Wind." The sad monotony experienced in "The New Sense" is precisely the monotony that belongs to the fusion of time, and it is because of the fusion that a new sense is needed to propel us into creativity.

The first three quatrains of "The New Sense" develop the feeling of monotony. Then EGM uses a transitional device, as he frequently does in series of quatrains, that serves to balance the second part of the poem with the first.[3]

The last three stanzas first reiterate the feeling of monotony by using imagery that could indicate newness—only here newness is lost in repetition. It is in the following stanza that the poet wishes specifically for an additional sense that would give things "unexpected forms and new lights" (*formas inesperadas y lumbres misteriosas*). (II.80) And in the last stanza we feel vividly the creative longing to be aware, in every act, in every emotion, of reality as if it were in the context of life at the beginning. Everything would be seen as new.

An approximation of this state occurs in "Exalted Afternoon" ("Tarde suprema"), a vibrant poem of both resignation and expectation. The quality of the emotion is established in the first stanza by use of color imagery that describes an afternoon undeniably beautiful and joyful. The feeling of the poem is then expressed in three actions of the soul. First, we sense the relationship of soul to setting. It is the soul that sees, not the eyes. Then the soul rejects the past, in a stanza that recalls "New Soul" from *Parables*. It is the soul that

> . . . hears the savage
> sonata of the squall with which the oak
> shakes and ennobles its branches.
>
> (. . . *siente la salvaje*
> *sonata del turbión con que la encina*
> *sacude y ennoblece su ramaje.*) (II.81)

The third action of the soul occurs at the end of the poem and communicates the combination of resignation and expectation. The experience has been so complete

> that the soul controls its deep yearning
> and, mistress now of the world's emotion,
> closes its eyes to await death.
>
> (*que el alma doma su anhelar profundo,*
> *y, dueña ya de la emoción del mundo,*
> *cierra los ojos a esperar la muerte.*) (II.82)

The death referred to here is certainly death as the fruition of life. It is an ecstatic resignation.

"Bedazzled Pilgrim" ("El romero alucinado") is the poem that gave the title to EGM's next volume. It is also concerned with the problem of time, and its fundamental question is whether the searcher (the pilgrim) is aware of time or of the road ahead. The poem is characterized by a refrain that is used with reference to morning, afternoon, and night. The refrain is a good enough device to give the poem structure, but it also produces a certain jauntiness that runs contrary to the serious intent of the piece. The intensity of the poet's feeling calls for a rather complicated statement, as in "House With Two Doors" ("Casa con dos puertas"). This poem is particularly interesting because of the amplification of its communication with the reader when it is read in the context of this volume. The reference to the time problem—which is really the high point of the poem and which comes right at the end—is so subtle that when the poem stands by itself, it may appear enigmatic, or may even be lost. Within the volume, it is a beautiful contribution to our total emotion.

"House With Two Doors" establishes, in the first stanza, the image of the poet's heart as a house which has sometimes been full of guests, but has more often been empty. As we follow the image into the second stanza, we discover that the guests are dreams—dreams that have come easily and stayed only a short time. In this stanza we have a strong feeling of disappointment, of unrealized hopes. The feeling is augmented in the third stanza where the poet recalls that generally the guests left little for those that were to come later. But the depression is lightened somewhat in the fourth stanza by the assurance that most guests did leave some small, positive indication of their visit. Then in the fifth and final stanza, the poet shifts from the past tense to the present tense, in order to capture the moment of the poetic experience, which has to come in silence. Within this stanza, the unknown guest is, in fact, the resplendent moment of this very poem. But we are not sure whether it comes from recalling something experienced (old sorrow) or from the persistence of an unrealized opportunity (tired love).

> And my cowardly disquiet asks
> if it is a tired love arrived late
> or an old sorrow never departed.

> (*Y se pregunta mi inquietud cobarde*
> *si es un cansado amor que llegó tarde*
> *o es un viejo dolor que no ha salido.*) (II.103)

An excellent example of the creation of the moment while using the past tense is "Sea Twilight" ("Crepúsculo marino"). If this poem were nothing else, it would be a magnificent word painting of a sunset. But it is more than that: both poet and reader respond, and the intimate emotion joins with the sunset so positively that we feel communion with the universe as strongly here as anywhere in EGM's poetry. He produces the effect mainly by use of the color red. Emanating from the sun and first coloring the heavens, red becomes the common characteristic of all creation. The soul contrasts through its whiteness, and is an ecstatic, counterpointing participant in the oneness of everything. The poem reaches its climax at the very end, as we feel the process of life being spent out, in the image of the bleeding heart: "and the profound life beat like a slow/ and bleeding heart" (*y la vida profunda latía como un lento/ y ensangrentado corazón*). (II.93)

"Carmine Uncertainty" ("Ventura carmina") develops from an emotional set related to the feeling of "Sea Twilight." Here we wonder what the "expected song" will be like when it comes. The basic question is whether it will be "like a trumpet at dawn" (*un clarín en la alborada*). (II.96) The development of the poem is a series of speculations on what else the song might be like, all of them based on the poet's communication with the world about him. Each speculation involves a kind of sound and a corollary emotion. But the next to the last stanza somewhat fearfully supposes that the song may be soundless, that it may be neither heard nor understood. And the end of the poem is the wish that it would be like the trumpet of dawn. Here is the desire for certainty, for renewal, in a circumstance that would promise the reunion captured in "Sea Twilight."

The merit of the persistent quest of knowing is expressed in the exhortation of "The Parade" ("El desfile"); it is more than a moral lesson, for here the exhortation is to the poet's heart: "Bleed, my heart . . ." ("*Sangra, corazón mío*"). (II.113) The imagery is intense and exciting, and we join with the poet in feeling the need to live fully. In a way, the poem is a justification of the strenuous search for deep communion even when we know the ultimate cannot be achieved. The image of the bleeding heart expresses the unreserved use of life.

> And while the tragedy of the years goes by,
> bleed, my heart, with your reddest blood.
>
> (*Y mientras la tragedia de los años desfila,*
> *sangra, corazón mío, con tu sangre más roja.*) (II.113)

II   Bedazzled Pilgrim

The physical appearance of the poems in this volume, published in 1923, comes as something of a surprise to EGM's reader. Many of them are short, some have only a few lines; and exterior form is noticeably irregular. In reading a few of the short pieces, we notice two unusual characteristics: one is that the poet frequently speaks of things that are associated with the details of daily life and sometimes uses a term that refers to modern technology; the other is that the poet appears to be detached from what he is observing. Perhaps vanguardism has invaded the poetic world of González Martínez. Glancing rapidly through the volume, we see that still a number of the poems look rather traditional and suspect that we have a two-pronged collection. The presence of other poems that are obviously inspired by the South American landscape suggests that we may have even a third group. Only a close examination of the volume will reveal the relationship that holds all the poems together. EGM is still the man in the midst of his search, still probing, still trying to see more deeply. At this point, he is much inclined to take account of himself, and frequently what he sees in the world amazes him. The landscape poems are observations translated into emotion. The shorter poems, even though many of them are detached from the poet, are no less observations; and generally speaking, they are attempts to see reality in a slightly different perspective. When the poet's emotion is not actually expressed within the poem, it is close by the side of it, and often we know that the poet is remarking what an extraordinary world this is. It is the bedazzled pilgrim who speaks.

"The Pilgrim's Three Things" ("Las tres cosas del romero"), the poem that opens this volume, is a sequel to "The Bedazzled Pilgrim" which was published in *Word of the Wind* and furnished the title for this later collection. Like the parent poem, "The Pilgrim's Three Things" is a bouncy piece that hardly does justice to the author's serious intent. The rhythm completely dominates the imagery in an explanation of how the pilgrim is equipped and what he must do. His three things are "his eyes open to the distance/an attentive ear and a quick step" (*los ojos abiertos a la lejanía/atento el oído y el paso ligero*). (II.137) Anyone who has read EGM's poetry knows well enough what the pilgrim is supposed to do with his tools. The image of the pilgrim is, of course, a reference to the individual's passage through life, but we can be reasonably certain that its use at this particular point in the author's poetic trajectory was prompted by his travel to and in Chile and Argentina, his first experience outside Mexico.

A tone of explanation pervades "The Pilgrim's Three Things," but an expansion of its theme in "The Unconscious Journey" ("La jornada inconsciente") loses the purely expository effect and becomes more creative within the poem itself. In an earlier poem we felt a moment of rejection of the quest of knowing, and substituted for it a purely sensory—perhaps emotional—communication. Here the poet is resigned to not knowing but persistent in the quest and in the expression of it: ". . . I only sing without knowing anything" (. . . *Canto no más sin saber nada*). (II.139) Still he gives us a feeling of certainty that someday what now is obscure will be clearly seen:

> but the day
> when I review my journey alone
> this golden vision will be mine . . .
>
> *(pero el día*
> *en que repase a solas mi jornada,*
> *esta visión dorada será mía . . .)* (II.139)

Just as "An Unconscious Journey" is an activation of the theory set forth in "The Pilgrim's Three Things," "A Phantom" ("Una fantasma") continues the thread of feeling, in a different way. It is the creation of the moment when knowledge (in this case, knowledge of the great beyond) is almost in the grasp of the poet, but then eludes him. The poem is an enigmatic, silent interview between the poet and a man who has returned from the dead. Both are speechless. The poet is aware that his companion knows answers to his questions, but the desire to ask the questions diminishes and the phantom disappears, leaving nothing but the most tangible reality.

Often we have felt with EGM the impossibility of knowing ultimate reality, and more than once we have felt with him that it should be that way. But no amount of resignation can end the yearning, or the feeling of incompleteness. "Someone Has Gone Away" ("Alguien se ha ido") is a different development of the need to reunite, because the perspective is different. Here the point of view is the poet's state of apartness, of his being separated from something that was part of himself. His statement is highly communicative because the poem develops the emotion gradually until we feel the anticipation of reunion as strongly as we feel the separation.

The development of the poem is based on its first line: "Someone or something has gone away" (*Alguien o algo se ha ido*).

(II.142) The poet then reasonably justifies the feeling by saying that otherwise he would not feel "this unfathomable vagueness of absence" (*esta insondable vaguedad de ausencia*). (II.142) The first stanza ends with an emphatic restatement of the basic proposition, but the "something" is lost in the restatement and only the "someone" remains. The second stanza wonders when the separation occurred, but this contemplative question is really a digression, because the circumstances of the separation are not important here. In the third stanza the poet says flatly that he will never know when or where or who it was that went away. Then he reviews the basic feeling of loss by saying he knows that someone responds to his song.

The hope of reunion appears in the last stanza. Here the poet directly addresses the lost "someone" as "disoriented being" (*desorientado ser*), (II.142) and hopes that it will return to its center. Then the expression of hope is reinforced:

> And the anguish of waiting that I carry inside me
> sees in the omens of the moon
> the fantastic token of the meeting.
>
> (*Y el ansia de esperar que llevo adentro,*
> *atisba en los presagios de la luna*
> *el fantástico signo del encuentro.*) (II.142)

The meaning of this poem comes mainly from four factors: the stark simplicity of the basic proposition, the suggestive quality of "this unfathomable vagueness of absence," the identification of "someone" as "disoriented being," and the intuited certainty of the last three lines, which are quoted above.

In "The Song" ("El canto"), EGM wants to find the meaningful, enduring expression, and he wants it so intensely that we feel a rush of impatience. The feeling is so strong that we tend to read the poem aloud; the sheer force of it is likely to make the reader stand if he is sitting, because it is a kind of impatience that requires some immediate change. Not only does the poet have trouble seeing as deeply as he wishes, he also finds it impossible to say the sort of thing he wants to say. Of course, the seeing and the saying are really not separate acts, because the saying produces song. So when we feel the need to sing the universal song, we are also feeling the need of universal identification. When, in the last stanza, the poet would silence the "unsonorous message" (*mensaje insonoro*), (II.154) he is also longing for more complete communion with the universe.

Still, in spite of not being able to sing the song he wants most to sing, the poet finds that he has not been allowed to give the best that he has to offer. In "The Knapsack" ("La alforja")—notice that the title carries out the pilgrim imagery—there is a deep feeling of desolation caused by awareness that men have taken what the poet's heart poured out, but have not waited to participate in the best. He is deserted, stands in coldness and isolation.

González Martínez continues to take account of himself in terms of the fusion of time, and still communicates a feeling of astonishment when a present circumstance suggests one from the past and, consequently, an old emotion lives in the present. This phenomenon appears in "Subtle Threads" ("Hebras sutiles"), but the poem is distinguished from others that are thematically similar, by the physical picture that triggers the emotion. The specific detail of the picture is like some of the short poems of this volume, but "Subtle Threads" is charged with emotion, and we are reminded of some of the poems of Ramón López Velarde. We have a mixed feeling of the rightness of things, and the reaction resembling stage fright that we are likely to feel on those great occasions that mark the passing of our years.

The studded church door
that bears a set of masks
from whose set grin
hang knockers
that no one has used,
and morning in the rain, remind me of
another morning like this, of the rainy season,
and of first communion,
when a rented coach and an umbrella,
with its bourgeois and paternal blackness,
protected the premature anxiety
of my troubled heart
(and the gold-encrusted candle,
tied
with the classic ribbon).

(La iglesia de portón claveteado
y que sostiene un par de mascarones
de cuyo rictus inmovilizado
penden aldabones
que nadie ha tocado,

> *y la mañana en lluvia, me recuerdan*
> *otra mañana así, de tiempo de aguas*
> *y de primera comunión,*
> *cuando un coche de punto y un paraguas,*
> *con su burguesa y paternal negrura,*
> *resguardaron el ansia prematura*
> *del desasosegado corazón*
> *[y la vela de cera escarchada,*
> *atada*
> *con el clásico listón].) (II.157)*

The poet is astonished here, facing the phenomenon of recall, just as he is in the other observations of life in the short poems of this volume.

"Street Musicians at Midnight" ("Murga de media noche"), like "Subtle Threads," captures the reality of a moment, makes a transition to the emotion evoked, and comments on the emotion. EGM stabilizes the happening, imprisons it as if it were a snapshot, by making a series of observations that emphasize substantives and minimize articles and finite verbs. The effect is of being awakened suddenly, of dimly recognizing the intruding noise, of being quite separated from the confusion in the street. The sleep itself has been dreamless, a vacuum. In the second stanza, the noise that replaced the suspension of sleep fades into the distance, and we feel a desire to dream something that would not be a vacuum at all, but would fulfill life. The poet communicates the purity of the possible dream by reference to a naked child. But in the third stanza, all that remains is the echo of the street musicians and life readjusts itself to this exterior reality. The moment, now lost, will join many others that move the author to ask "Where is life that I may crush it in my arms?" (*¿En dónde está la vida para ahogarla en mis brazos?*), (II.66) as the first line of "The Tragic Hour" ("La hora trágica").

Bedazzled Pilgrim contains one poem that carries a question mark for its title because it is a consideration of the conflict between continuity and change in the individual. This conflict is often related to the fusion of time in EGM's poetic discovery, but here it stands out more clearly as an unresolvable conflict. Five of the poem's six quatrains develop the feeling of constant change. They move from the specific concept of today's man being a different man tomorrow, to the idea of a constant flow of time, "this incessant becoming" (*este incesante devenir*),

(II.172) in which the moment arrives but is in the process of leaving, even as it reaches us. The sixth stanza appears in parentheses, indicating that the poet considers the development of the poem already complete. This parenthetical stanza is a reluctance to accept the condition described in the first five, because the poet feels intuitively that something is durable and always remains. He reinforces this feeling, of course, in those poems—"Subtle Threads," for example—that are based on what we may call the retrospective emotion. But in many other poems, as in "Strange Bondage," he senses the meaning of the past within the constant flow. He is surprised by the presence of the past, and not always pleasantly so. Certainly in "The Useless Days" he would prefer to be freed by the certainty of change, and "The New Sense" is obviously a yearning for the state of incessant becoming. The new landscape of South America was appealing for his not having experienced it; in the poet's quest for communion, it provided new suggestion. It was something like seeing the world again and, in this respect, is similar to the short poems that place the world in a strange perspective.

The first instance in EGM's poetry of a specific mention of the modern world about him is "Radiogram" ("Radiograma"). But we see immediately that his use of this technological miracle is different from the typically vanguardist intention of discovering beauty in all these modern things. EGM's poetry is not here, nor did it ever become, the song of the powerful, roaring machine. In this poem the radiogram serves only as an image for expressing an emotion which is very frequently felt in the poetry of González Martínez: the silence of the stars communicates with the poet. Here the poet appears as the pilgrim, and his soul is the antenna that receives the message of light and silence. Beginning with the song of a single star, the poet then incorporates all the stars in such a way that our reaction is to the universal song. The imagery of the radiogram is carried out faithfully through the entire poem; but as is often the case with EGM's images, the physical characteristic of the image is dominated by the emotion that it creates.

We must be careful in saying that EGM's use of modern things is not typical of vanguardist usage because, although the statement is true enough, it would be wrong to give the impression that he was not motivated by the new poetry. Indeed, the probability is that he did become interested in the modern things via his acquaintance with Vanguardism, but he used them in his own way. We may also suppose that his experiments in poetic form were inspired by his observation of the new poetry. The form of "Radiogram" is irregular, though it certainly would not be considered radical as compared with other poetry of the time. The poet uses assonantal rather than complete rhyme, and the line lengths vary. They are rhythmic, but not in the traditional sense. Some lines are extremely short.

> A star sings
> in the heavens
> its sonata
> of light and silence.
>
> *(Una estrella canta*
> *en el cielo*
> *su sonata*
> *de luz y silencio.)* (II.177)

The enclosing first and last lines balance each other, as do the middle two, but much the same effect would be produced if the stanza were written as a couplet, rather than as a quatrain. The placement in four lines does change the rhythm ever so slightly, and therefore increases the weight of the impression made by the nouns of the two middle lines.

Much more interesting than experimentation with form is EGM's point of view which often implies, even if it does not state, the poet's astonishment before the world. He examines and reports small incidents and objects, even emotions, as if a part of the world's reality were under a poetic microscope. Even when the emotion itself is contained within the poem, it receives a kind of clinical treatment. It is not that these poems do not communicate, but that the feeling is different from walking with the author in the endless quest. Here the quest continues, but we stand now by the poet's side, bedazzled by all there is.

"Newton's Apple" ("La manzana de Newton") relates the event of a boy's death when he falls out of a tree. The statement is so coldly factual that this piece is almost prose. After we know that the boy falls, the poem shifts to very short lines to emphasize the disaster. Here the poet uses details that communicate the horror of the child's death, and the short lines have something of the quality of a sensationalist news report. The arrangement of the short lines adds emphasis to certain words as in "Radiogram." The emotional impact of the poem, however, depends on the last lines which, in spite of being as matter of fact as the rest of the poem, deliver the flood of emotion at the end.

> Tomorrow there will be no classes in the town school.
> Let all the youngsters know.
>
> (*Mañana no habrá clases en la escuela del pueblo.*
> *Que avisen a todos los chicos.*) (II.200)

We have a feeling of being separated from the event, even of seeing it objectively. When we first feel the emotion at the end, it is with a kind of objective sympathy that exacts no personal grief from us. But then the emotional wave strikes again, and we know that what this event really amounts to is the moment when the thing that we usually call life disappears. We feel the tragedy of not being involved.

"The Skylight" ("El tragaluz") serves the single purpose of communicating the poetic emotion. Clouds frame an airplane stunting high above (the "modern" reference again), and there is a sudden rush of hope. But this is an enigmatic poem because there is no development that leads to the concluding emotion; and although the imagery is attractive, we have no way of moving into the feeling expressed by the poet at the end. There are other poems that, with no expression of emotion at all, manage to evoke a strong reaction through the sheer strength of the imagery. "Black Mass" ("Misa negra") is pure imagery— six lines, with a final couplet reinforcing the quatrain. The scene is the silhouette of a church, and we imagine two towers because the poet sees in it the sign of the cuckold: index finger and little finger pointing upward, with the two middle fingers held down by the thumb. The church is mentioned in the first line, then the next three say nothing of the church, but describe the cuckold sign in detail. The effect is so well balanced that we see alternating flashes of the sign and the silhouette. The two points of a new moon, in the couplet, complete the picture and make the impression insistent.

When we read these impression poems of González Martínez, it is well to remember that some vanguardist poets were attracted by Japanese *haiku*. Only rarely did they closely approximate the form or spirit of classical *haiku*, but their partial appreciation of the Japanese genre influenced them to esteem short poetry based on an isolated image.[4] Very few of EGM's poems—none

of these that we are considering at this point—could be called
haiku, because the personal emotion is generally too much in
evidence. It would be only when he felt in closest communion
with the universe that EGM would approximate *haiku.* And, of
course, there is the question of form. Most of his poems, even
the short ones, are far too long to qualify. Still it seems probable
that his tendency to isolate the image is related to the similar
interest found among other poets of the time. Many of EGM's
short pieces indicate that he is following a process of looking
deeply, and this deeper vision almost always evokes the poet's
reaction. In "The Fly" ("La mosca"), for example, the last two
lines reveal an important aspect of the poet's way of thinking.

> The fly
> with stubborn courage beats
> on the same place in the glass
> of the closed window . . .
> If he were to live a thousand years,
> he would open the desired breach.
> A fly is more than a drop,
> and a drop carves out stone.

> *(La mosca*
> *con terca intrepidez golpea*
> *en el mismo punto del vidrio*
> *de la cerrada vidriera . . .*
> *Si viviera mil años,*
> *abriría la deseada brecha.*
> *Una mosca es más que una gota,*
> *y una gota cava la piedra.)* (II.195)

Some of the short poems reveal an oblique view of reality,
and they are humorous not so much because the author wants
them to be so, as because they turn out that way when EGM
puts a scene in a different perspective. In "Elephantine Dance"
("Danza elefantina"):

The elephant, when he dances,
loses his monumental gravity.
One might say that an earthquake moves
the four columns with which he establishes himself on the ground . . .
He makes me think of the shadow of Johann Sebastian Bach
playing a modern tango on the organ.

(El elefante, cuando baila,
pierde su gravedad de monumento.

Se diría que un terremoto desquicia
las cuatro columnas con que se afinca al suelo . . .
Me parece la sombra de Juan Sebastián Bach
ejecutando al órgano algún tango moderno.) (II.201)

Amusing as these poems are, they are undoubtedly the expression of a perfectly serious man who is facing the astonishing world. The reaction is not always the same, and can well vary from pain to joy. "Two Instants" ("Dos instantes") is a set of contrasting short poems that show these extremes, and the poet enters, parenthetically, at the end of each of the two stanzas to make sure that the two reactions are clearly exposed.

III   Subtle Tokens

The playful mood of some of the poems of *Subtle Tokens* (1925) runs contrary to the sense of foreboding that emanates from others. We have a feeling of desperately holding on, of putting the best foot forward, while anticipating disaster. This foreboding is related to death, but its quality may be better described if we say that it is caused by the seeping away of life. In "Broken Amphora" ("Anfora rota"), life is like a vessel that has been cracked, but the perfume of its contents now comes through the cracks. This rather gentle optimism takes on a feeling of desperation in "Ballad of the Mad Fortune" ("Balada de la loca fortuna"):

> With the sun, the sea, the wind, and the moon
> I am going to amass a mad fortune.

> *(Con el sol, el mar, el viento y la luna*
> *voy a amasar una loca fortuna.)* (II.233)

In this ebullient mood, the poet promises to make very appealing uses of the things of nature (gold coins from the sun, etc.), but will keep the moon in his heart. The joyful rhythm of the piece deserves a tune. At the other extreme, "The Token" ("La señal") captures a moment of augury when the communication between poet and star informs him of "a date for the not too distant future" (*una cita para no muy tarde*). (II.259) The author is also hypersensitive to the death of other people, as in "Bitter Day" ("Día aciago") which creates the effect of a major sadness. The emotion derives from news of the death of the friend about whom he dreamed last night. This circumstance involves the life-death contrast, the continuity-change puzzle; and the appearance of the world is entirely different, everything is clouded. We feel that perhaps the anguish came ahead of the news. We must not understand, however, that EGM has given up the attempt to see deeply. Rather than the communion with all things that is his method of seeing in much of his poetry, the technique in *Subtle Tokens* is the fragment of experience placed in a perspective that gives it a new appearance, the same technique that we find so often in *Bedazzled Pilgrim*. Even the longer poems, both the rollicking ones and the foreboding ones, tend to look at life this way. And as is also the case in *Bedazzled Pilgrim*, many of the pieces are short. The two collections are really companion volumes.

Sometimes the short poems deal only with the emotion itself. Rather than produce an emotion by viewing an object or an event, the poem views the emotion. "Gentle Madness" ("La apacible locura") carries a feeling of renewal, but the emotion is kept "in the dark prison of my bewitched heart" (*en la cárcel oscura del embrujado corazón*). (II.228) "The Enigma" ("El enigma") communicates the emotion in an entirely different way. The first two of its four lines say simply that a voice sounds in the middle of the night. The last two lines are exclamations that express hope that the source of the voice may remain secret. The first of the exclamations refers specifically to the voice, but the second enlarges the voice to the "mystery of the woods" (*misterio del bosque*). (II.229) This enlargement opens the way for the emotional reaction, and it expands to include all that is implied by EGM's references to the ultimate secret. The search that is life depends on the protection of the secret—a feeling made completely clear in "The Guardian" ("El guardián").

Subtle Tokens contains more poems that create the pure experience—that is, with no emotion suggested within the poem itself—than the preceding volume. "Return" ("Retorno") is based on an automobile ride at night. It is a series of images that suggest fatigue, boredom, and which end with the poet counting lights as he passes. The feeling of interminableness reaches its height when the counting by numbers turns into "and another . . . and another . . . and another . . ." (*y otro . . . y otro . . . y otro . . .*). (II.265) "The Strike" ("La huelga") is a similar event. The feeling of the city, completely altered by a general strike, is funereal. The emotion is contained within the circumstance. One of the most effective pieces of this kind creates a great deal of local Mexican color, an unusual thing for EGM. The poem, "Nectar of Apam" ("Néctar de Apam"), starts with the gaudiness of a pulque shop and enlarges the image to include the bullfight in such a way that one is not separated from the other. The poem as a whole could be described as a feeling of Mexico; but it contains more than the feeling suggested by the image, because the last line refers to four centuries of suffering and silence.

One of the poet's techniques in the short pieces is the suppression of finite verbs. In "The Nest" ("El nido") and "Wireless" ("T.S.H."), he uses a verbless observation and then asks a question. These poems are the most frugal of EGM's works; they also show very clearly the reaction of the poet to the phenomenon observed, without defining the emotion.

Wireless
telegraphy . . .
What about the birds
that write the music of the roads? . . .

(Telegrafía
sin hilos . . .
¿Qué va a ser de los pájaros
que anotan la música de los caminos? . . .) (II.277)

The poet's intention of seeing the world in a different way is clearly expressed in "While the Rain Falls" ("Mientras la lluvia cae"). This poem is, to a considerable extent, an explanation of the kind of poetry—or perhaps better, of the point of view—that appears in this collection. It is a little surprising that this particular poem is rather traditional. In the first lines, the poet rests his head and his sorrow against the glass of a window which "is weeping tears of pure water" (*llora lágrimas de agua pura*). (II.266) The physical reality of the poet is associated with his emotional reality from the start. The distortion caused by the water makes the poet see a distorted world—the world is "sickened" (*enferma*), II.266, by the distortion. This world in caricature is described in the second stanza. The new vision is associated with the poet's grief, but he knows that the sun will restore a healthier reality. Still he must record the experience of the new view.

In the midst of these poems that try valiantly to see what the world really is, EGM offers to bet his heart that the world and the heart will never understand each other. In "Wager" ("Apuesta"), the world wants noise, movement, the modern things: (*El quiere jazz-band . . ./y tango y shymmy y one-step*); (II.242) the heart sings silently. In "Noli me tangere" he withdraws into himself, keeping his soul inviolate, protecting what must always be his own: "Touch not my soul,/ because you would crush it" (*No me toques el alma,/ porque la estrujarías*). (II.279) Here again is the integrity of silence, the weeping that cannot be heard—if there is weeping. Here too is the enigma. And the poem radiates the gentleness of EGM that always appears when he is most aware of his own reality.

Caught between past and present, the poet is in the middle of life. He recognizes his condition in "Password" ("Santo y seña") when he is halted and challenged by an unidentified voice. He is confused and cannot think of the reply. He cannot go forward, nor can he go back. In the third and last stanza, he asks his companion if by chance she knows the password. We have no reason to think she does except that she has been with him many years. Perhaps she is the soul, perhaps the beloved—perhaps she is both.

CHAPTER 4

The Poetry of Sorrow

When my footsteps,
hastened by absence . . .
—"Last Journey"

I Unfinished Poems

TEN years passed before the publication of another volume of poetry—the only lapse of any consequence in EGM's poetic trajectory. We cannot forget that the poet, in the pieces published in 1925, was acutely aware of the uncertainties that arose from his being caught in the middle of life. He was not at all sure of the validity of his poetic road, and he was asking questions. It is well to remember also that the new poetry of the time was very different from the poetry that had influenced his own formation. The poetry of the vanguardists had certainly affected the work of EGM, but there is no reason to think that it illuminated his path. On the contrary, the vanguardist effect on his vision was to intensify his reaction of astonishment without contributing to the communion that the poet sought. The questions multiplied, and the answers were as elusive as ever.

In the unpoetic world, González Martínez devoted himself to being a good diplomat, and his success is at least partially indicated by the elevation of the Mexican representation in Spain to the status of Embassy. His understanding of the immediate condition of society is also seen in his 1925 address on Mexican problems.[1] This kind of concern was to find its poetic expression eventually in three long poems based on society rather than on the individual.

When the poet-diplomat returned to Mexico in 1931, he was the dean of Mexican poets. In spite of the fact that he was not inclined by his own nature or by his poetic impulse to be the leader of literary groups or schools, he was an inspiration to the younger poets because of his poetic and human integrity.

He was not drawn into the activity of the hectic literary world,[2] but there can be no doubt that EGM's calm, unpretentious, universal outlook contributed much to the maintenance of artistic validity in Mexican poetry. Still it was four years before the publication of *Unfinished Poems* (*Poemas truncos*) in 1935, the year that also brought the death of the poet's wife.

No doubt EGM wished to indicate a change in his psychic state when, in arranging the poems for this volume, he chose "Maturity" ("Madurez") as the opening piece. It is not the kind of poem that progressively implicates the reader in the poetic act; rather, it is a simple statement that elicits our sympathetic understanding of the poet's position. Essentially, he is the same man he has always been, but now, ten years later, he is calmer, less anxiety ridden. The statement is made in three stanzas, in three sets of images of diminishing scope. The first set is general: the sea quiets, the wind calms down, the soul steadies, the sword is sheathed.

The second set of images refers specifically to the poet's acts. We feel the new calmness through the change from "imprecation" (*imprecación*) to "prayer" (*rezo*). (III.7) The use of "imprecation" must be understood in the light of the rest of the stanza, where he refers to the flight of his "anxieties" (*ansias*); his imprecation was not in the nature of a curse, but is the way he chooses to describe the pressure he felt in the poetic search. We will see a reflection of this sentiment in "Which is Better?" ("¿Qué será mejor?"), a poem that makes us feel that the intensive search may not be fair to others, and this doubt is related to the ego problem considered in "Meditation Under the Moon." In "Maturity," the feeling of pressure is reinforced by reference to the past as a "mad time" (*loco tiempo*). (III.7)

In the third stanza, the scope of the imagery is further reduced and refers to the poet's eye. Here we also feel a decrease of anxiety—the gleam is diminished; but the searching eye keeps on observing, and takes in more. The final line of the poem expresses happiness with the new state of maturity. "Duality" ("Dualidad") concentrates on the act of seeing, and defines it in such a way that there can be no doubt of the poet's continued search. The basis of the imagery is the dual function, within the poet, of Narcissus and Argos (the one of the hundred eyes). The sense of the poem is the combination of seeing within ourselves and outside ourselves at the same time. The structure of

the poem is like "Maturity" in that the point is made by three
stanzas which are on the same plane, but the imagery differs
in size or scope from stanza to stanza. Each set of images presents
the double vision of self and other. The first is cosmic in its
reach, the second refers to specific things (a drop, a bell), and
the third personalizes the emotion so that it belongs to poet
and reader. The involvement of the reader is greatly increased
by EGM's use, in the last stanza, of the "we" and "us" forms.

"Victory Over Time" ("Victoria sobre el tiempo") is an exultant poem by the poet father of a poet son.[3] The essence of the
feeling is contained in the opening lines of the two stanzas:
"Finally life is mine" (*Por fin la vida es mía*) and "Today I have
conquered time" (*Hoy he vencido al tiempo*). (III.11) In the
imagery of passing on the torch, we share a sense of relief in
knowing that there will be continuity. The expectation is expressed in the last two lines:

> A voice, in the flight of years,
> is to finish the stanza I began!

> (*Una voz, en la fuga de los años,*
> *ha de acabar la comenzada estrofa!*) (III.11)

These few lines, very simple but very joyful, are extremely
poignant in the light of "Last Journey" ("Ultimo Viaje"), a
beautiful poem written on the death of the poet son. But "Victory
Over Time" is by itself an expression of perfect joy.

EGM communicates the joy of maturity beautifully in "Aban-
don ("Abandono"), a poem of superb contentment—not the
satisfaction of perfect accomplishment, but of dignified renunciation. He makes excellent use of phrases in which specific actions
communicate the mood, and which use noun verbals rather than
finite verbs: "A falling of apples" (*Un caer de manzanas*).
(III.18) The poem builds a general feeling of autumn and of
quiet. Throughout the poem there is an awareness that what
the poet is feeling may have a wider significance than it has
for him, and it is before this possibility that the renunciation
takes place.

We experience a feeling of spiritual communion in "Shadows"
("Sombras"), where everything—universe and time—appears to
be joined. The shadows speak with the soul, but not audibly.
What they say is the soul's business; indeed, the shadows are
so much a part of the soul, that even when the soul is among

them, it is alone rather than accompanied. Somewhere, however, there is a counting off, a marking, an awareness of time as a series of instants. The sense of reunion emanates even more vividly from "New Soul" ("Alma Nueva"). This "New Soul" is different from the poem by the same title that was published in "Parables," but there is an interesting relationship. The poetic yearning, in the earlier poem, is to be the throbbing heart of the universe, to be pure emotion. That state is very nearly what happens in the present poem, and the insight is a little startling. The poetic tools are the eyes, and they have become many-faceted, so seeing in many directions at once.

> Images once confused
> and in a succession of moments,
> now become simultaneous for me
> and perfectly clear.
>
> *(Imágenes antes confusas*
> *y en sucesión de momentos,*
> *hoy se me vuelven simultáneas*
> *y de contornos perfectos.)* (III.65)

It is important to note that not only has there been a joining of what was seen separately, but also that in the unified state, reality has taken on a clarity it did not have before. The rest of the imagery reinforces this feeling of revelation. Then the poet wonders where the new soul has come from. Finally, he notes that the clock has not moved for some time. This final line intensifies the state of suspension.

The quality of the poetic vision finds its expression in a feeling of clarity, of transparency. Several poems communicate the satisfaction of insight, in imagery that challenges us to look. Associations with morning produce this effect of clarity and purity; suggestions of the movement of air take us forward; colors, although they are not necessarily pastel, suggest seeing through the color itself. There is an intense feeling of openness, of receptivity. "Nakedness" ("Desnudez") has, perhaps, the most complete development of the poems that communicate this expectancy.[4] Its short lines enhance the feeling of anticipation, but it is not an anguished waiting and does not in any way contradict the calmness that maturity has brought the poet.

At the beginning of the poem, the effect of morning is felt in a "Clean and blue drop" (*Gota limpia y azul*), (III.20) that changes slightly the direction of the poet's yearning. The air is so quiet and so of itself (that is, the air has the absolute quality of being only itself and completely itself) that "the soul is immersed in the soul" (*el alma se ahoga en el alma*). (III.20) Here is the Narcissus facet of "Duality." Then the Argos facet appears, not in an active way, but as receiver. A song is heard from afar. The poet's solitude, specifically, becomes the receiver, "stretched out on the wet grass/ naked to the sun and the wind" (*tendida en la hierba mojada,/ desnuda al sol y al viento*). (III.21) It is here that the anticipation becomes intense, while the poet's solitude awaits the response of "all the things of the world" (*todas las cosas del mundo*). (III.21)

In "Which Is Better?" EGM poses the problem of choosing between the active search for communion, and an innocent passivity. We are likely to feel in this poem the anxiety created by the difficulty of maintaining the intact life. It is composed entirely of questions, and we feel no accomplishment in any direction, only confusion. In "The Hammock" ("La hamaca"), however, the poet chooses the active road. The hammock image is similar to the pendulum. In the first part of the poem, its movement, which is the movement of his uncertainty, lulls him, suspends him over life, isolates him from commitment. But in the second part, a deep communication with nature—implied rather than developed in the poem—stirs the poet to activity and to the anticipation of a life of "love and sacrifice and endurance" (*amor, y sacrificio y reciedumbre*). (III.17)

The specific and positive ambition of the poet, of course, is to write the verse that will change men by bringing to them the full reality that the poet sees. In "Sound X" ("El sonido X") he longs for the day when he will be able to say more than words will say. Within the poem he tries to capture the feeling of what the new communication would be like, mostly through synesthetic imagery: "the echo of a fragrance" (*el eco de una fragrancia*), "the symphony of the sun on the beach (*la sinfonía del sol en la playa*). (III.26) At the end of the poem, he expresses his disgust with the inadequacy of words by calling them "treacherous and vile (*traicioneras y viles*). (III.26) "Prayer" ("Plegaria") is a forceful plea that the words of the poet be creative and have an effect among men. We should understand clearly that this poem has nothing to do with the role that the poet as a man fulfills in society; it is rather the

active role of the poet's word that is hoped for. In a series of
strong images, we feel the desire for men's vision to be less
limited. The poet would communicate his deep and extended
vision to all men. But the expression of this vision would be
different from the past because it would be more violent; and
indeed, this poem itself communicates that violence. And if the
poet's word cannot be the new voice that he would have it be,
he prays, just as in "Prayer of the Sterile Rock," that he be
granted "the sacred silence of stone" (*el sagrado mutismo de
la piedra*). (III.28)

Toward the end of *Unfinished Poems*, in the fourth part, we
find the reaction of the poet to the loss of the beloved. "Song
of Madness and Weeping" ("Canción de locura y llanto") is an
outpouring of grief in which life has lost all order, all rhythm.
There is no reason to suppress the violent emotion, no reason
to sing quietly, now that the beloved's absence has destroyed
the measure of life.

"In aeternum vale" is a more disciplined poem with an even
deeper expression of sorrow. Here the author turns to the sonnet,
and wisely so, because it is undoubtedly his best form. The
poem causes us to feel the beginning and end of the beloved's
presence, particularly in terms of the rhythm of life that was
her special gift to the poet. In this sonnet and in "Song of
Madness and Weeping," these suggestions of rhythm have something of the value of what we mean when we refer to the reason
for being. "In aeternum vale" uses two major images. One is
the first line, "In the introit of an auroral road" (*En el introito
de auroral camino*), (III.71) a very intense expression of beginning through the use of introit (the first part of the Mass) and
the suggestion of dawn. The second image, "white undulation
of linen" (*blanca ondulación de lino*), (III.71) is used in the
last line of the sonnet. The image refers to the quality of the
beloved. "Undulation" is related to the rhythm of life. The
suggested whiteness reinforces the purity of dawn in the first
image. And of course, the second image is a hypallage, since the
adjective "white" logically belongs to "linen" rather than to
"undulation." We cannot escape the association of white linen
with introit, and therefore, have an awareness of the sacrificial
aspect of the Mass.

"The Soul in Flight" ("El alma en fuga") is another sonnet,
this one communicating the anguish of loneliness. It is an

intensely personal poem, but not one that we are embarrassed to share. Indeed, the sonnet concludes with a plea for the support of others. In "Grief" ("Dolor"), again in sonnet form, the poet takes a first, tentative step toward the restoration of his emotional equilibrium. The first quatrain is a statement of the completeness of the poet's union with the beloved, a union so profound that, even as he writes, he is not really certain whether his own life continues to be life, or is death deceived into thinking it is life. The second quatrain recalls the beloved's death and the feeling of nothingness that was the poet's. The first tercet enlarges this feeling through the sense of a world disintegrating. But the second tercet makes a contrast when the poet observes the continuity of the things of nature. He recognizes that the world still is.

In the midst of his sorrow, the poet begins to ponder his own future. The loss of the beloved intensifies the questioning that had already become so prominent in his expression. "The New Journey" ("El nuevo viaje") is the conflict, in two stanzas, between not wanting to go on and the necessity of doing so. The development of the opposing feelings is based on the contrast between night and dawn.

"The Unfinished Journey" ("El viaje trunco") recaptures the sense of fulfillment of life with the beloved. Each of its stanzas, all quatrains, evokes emotion from some image associated with the search. The last verse asks, in a tone of innocent astonishment, what it was that interrupted the journey.

II   Absence and Song

There can be no doubt that EGM had by this time rediscovered the sonnet. In the first poem of this volume (1937), he writes a sonnet to the redemptive quality of poetry. "Poetry" ("Poesía") shows that the poetic act is more than a retreat, it is salvation. But not even poetry can change the author's new awareness of death. In "The Asp" ("El áspid") we are given a feeling of wariness, because death is lurking. This is a short poem, in six couplets. The first three tell, in the past tense, of the visit of death. The fourth changes from past to present to warn of the continued presence of death, and continues in an amplification of the warning. "The Night Serenaders" ("La ronda") is a more inviting, more substantial poem. The basic meaning is not at all hermetic: the poet's people are dying, the

ones that belonged to him; soon he too will die, and others will
ask the same questions he now asks, but will hear no answer.
The image of the street serenaders is basic to the development. The poem begins with both music and dance. It all comes
out of the past, the orchestra is of the dead. A Dance of Death
is performed by those who once were the people of EGM, but
now are separated from him. The second and third stanzas
develop this sense of separation. Then in the fourth stanza, the
poet knows that he will soon take his place among the senenaders
and will accommodate himself "to their rhythms" (*a sus ritmos*).
The use of rhythm here, as in other poems of these years, is a
reference to a characteristic of a state of being, and since he
would adjust to the rhythm of the serenaders, we know that he
expects a different mode of being.

"The Condemned" ("El condenado") is a series of twenty-
seven tercets, autobiographical and contemplative.

> I view and review on my deserted beach,
> my black rosary of fortune.
>
> (*paso y repaso en mi desierta playa*
> *mi camándula negra de fortuna.*) (III.83)

The poet then sets his mood of disillusionment or, at best, suspension, and builds the prelude to disappointment in the first
half of the poem.

> I am the one who once
> asked serenity of the stars . . .
> And here I am, still waiting!
>
> (*Yo soy aquél que un día*
> *pidió serenidad a las estrellas* . . .
> *¡Y aquí estoy, esperando todavía!*) (III.83)

Each tercet is a memory of some specific aspect of the poet's
desire to communicate with the life of things, to have the sense
of being one or another of the things he saw. We feel here his
creative urge, the reality of newness, of making, that would
come with the desired union. But he believes now that his poetic
quest was a mad flight. Then his reality, both past and present,
was illuminated by love; but that too vanished. At the end of
the poem, the artist stands as his own judge, and condemns
himself to not asking pardon for his madness and to die in
dungeons of silence. This is not the exalted silence of the sterile
rock, but the bitter silence of defeat.

Silence, however, is transformed by the poet's awareness of himself at a particular time, and it is capable of taking on a cosmic quality, as in "Vae soli," though its grandeur certainly does not in any way communicate satisfaction. The silence of this poem is the most absolute of any in EGM's poetry, and it communicates a frightening sense of loneliness. "Vae soli" begins with a simple statement of visible reality, limited in scope, which establishes a static condition and lays the perfect groundwork for the state of silence that the poem develops.

> The clock on the wall has stopped
> at five minutes of two . . .
>
> *(El reloj en el muro se ha parado*
> *a las dos menos cinco . . .)* (III.87)

The poet uses the present perfect tense to establish this positive, external fact, then changes to the present tense. The shift to the reality of silence is immediate, but is limited to the specific place.

> Silence of the bedroom,
> beside which all silence is noise!
>
> *(¡Silencio de la alcoba,*
> *junto del cual todo silencio es ruido!)* (III.87)

This description of silence gives it a special quality, as if it were the very essence of silence. In the second stanza, the scope of influence of silence is enlarged, and at the same time its terrible depth is reiterated.

> Even the sun is afraid of disturbing it
> when it sets fire to the soul of the window panes.
>
> *Hasta el sol tiene miedo de turbarlo*
> *al encender el alma de los vidrios.)* (III.87)

We have by this time entered completely into the feeling of the poet, for his imagery is no longer a description of what is happening around him, but an expression of his own emotion. The physical aspect of the sun image contributes to the setting: a place and a time of day. But the emotion is what the poet feels—not that the poet feels afraid, but that he feels the depth of silence that would evoke the image of the sun's fear. We experience the same kind of transfer from an invisible actor in the next image:

even sleep descends, with a finger
on its lips, for fear of wounding it. [the silence, that is]

(hasta el sueño desciende, con un dedo
sobre los labios, por temor de herirlo.) (III.87)

The all-pervading silence becomes primordial in the third stanza;
it is the "silence of the worlds/ recumbent in the bottom of the
abyss" (*silencio de los mundos/ yacentes en el fondo del abismo*).
(III.87) It is the silence that preceded sound. In the fourth
stanza it is the silence of space, which is cold and empty (the
opposite of EGM's vibrant participation). Silence is specifically
associated with solitude for the first and only time in the poem,
but this one instance is enough to underscore the awareness
that grows throughout these verses. And finally, it becomes not
only the silence of space, but the silence of time as well, for
centuries of centuries.

Wrapped in silence, the poet tries to recapture the meaning
of what he has experienced. In "Images" ("Imágenes"), memory
eludes him, experience is partial: "I seize the echo and lose the
cry" (*Atrapo el eco y se me pierde el grito*). (III.88) We have
the feeling of seeing the photographic negative of experience,
while groping for the positive. The poet himself compares it
to a reflection: "false disc of the moon in a mirror,/ green willow
with inverted branches" (*falso disco de luna en el espejo,/ verde
saúz de ramos invertidos*). (III.88) It has the feeling of a kind
of madness, and EGM calls it "the passion and death of Narcissus" (*la pasión y la muerte de Narciso*). (III.89)

The black night of "Nocturne" ("Nocturno"), with all its
frightening darkness, brings also the wisdom of silence. And
when, in this setting, the hours return, they have a fresh aspect.
Joy and sorrow come together, but silently. We feel an awareness of something that is very much ours, but still sufficiently
apart so that the emotions they evoke can be examined. It is
something like looking at old photographs.

In "Renunciation" ("Renunciación") the poet captures in his
words the feeling of a fundamental change in the nature of his
being. The words themselves do not explain the change, but
the new state is revealed. There are two long stanzas that develop
the feeling, and a short final stanza that amounts to a conclusion.
In the first, we feel the efforts of the poet to come to grips with
the physical facts of the universe, to find the relationship of
himself as man with the visible, created things around him. The

second stanza begins with the line that is the core of the poem: "I am no longer anything but a soul" (*Ya no soy sino un alma*). (III.99) We read the line as a proposition and continue then with the expression of the poet's renunciation of all that identifies him as a man of flesh and blood. The revelation of the new state is brought to a conclusion in the third stanza in words that communicate the sense of complete presentness, of being removed from time and from tangible things. The last line is a repetition of the key line of the poem, the one that begins the second stanza; but now it is different, for the tone of proposition has changed to one of explanation. After the first statement, the poet shows why the statement is true; but the second statement explains why the poet is as he is.

The poetic concentration is on the recovery of the beloved in "The Search" ("La búsqueda"). Concern for reunion with all things is subordinated to the need for reunion with the beloved.

> Wherever death hides
> you, I will look for you:
> through water, through fire,
> through the earth, through the air . . .
>
> (*Por doquiera que te esconda*
> *la muerte, voy a buscarte*:
> *por el agua, por el fuego,*
> *por la tierra, por el aire . . .*) (III.106)

The poet repeats this stanza at the end, and so frames a promise that he will look everywhere. He makes only one reservation:

> I will leave unsaid only your name
> so it may not escape me
> and I lose the only thing
> they have not been able to take from me . . .
>
> (*Solo callaré tu nombre*
> *para que no se me escape*
> *y se me pierda lo único*
> *que no han podido quitarme . . .*) (III.106)

The same passionate desperation is felt also in "Anniversary" ("Aniversario"), where the poet would immortalize the beloved, but cannot because words are inadequate. More than that, he searches for a way to retain what is escaping him, but there is no solution. His verse will not hold the reality.

III   Roses in the Amphora

This small collection of fifteen poems was published by the newspaper *El Nacional* in 1939 and included in the third volume of EGM's collected verse which appeared in 1940. In many ways, the poems resemble those of *Absence and Song*, but there is a greater range of emotion in these few poems, perhaps a result of the poet's working his way through to a comprehension of his new state. The first poem carries the title of the collection and sets the tone for the group. The three roses are grief, memory, and hope, but they only suggest the multitude of emotional shadings in the poems. We feel sorrow, in "Distances" ("Distancias"), become the beat of life, rather than the poet's personal affliction. "Eternal Sea" ("Mar eterno") communicates the poet's sorrow in sea imagery; and it is during this fantasy voyage that we see again the union of poet and beloved, as it was created in the resplendent moment of "The Sphinx," now on a desert island.

The overwhelming loneliness of "Eternal Sea" is placed in an unusual perspective in the sonnet "The Farewell" ("La despedida"). The poem is an anticipation of death, without the comfort of the one who has gone before. The vision of death has a certain quality of a time of beginning, but this suggestion of hope fades before the utter loneliness of the sonnet's sextet.

In "Phantom Ship" ("Bajel fantasma") we join the poet in feeling the inexorable course of life and man's frustration caused by lack of control over his destiny. We feel also the darkness of the way that is life, the absence of self-realization. But this description of the poem is the result of hindsight; it is what we see after reading all of it. The real value of its five quatrains is the gradual revelation throughout the course of the poem. The significance of EGM's imagery is not completely clear until the last line; meanwhile he controls the reader's emotional reaction very carefully.

The title itself is an integral part of the poem, because it suggests an allegory. The first words, "traveller shadows" (*sombras viajeras*), are followed immediately by a verb in the "we" form: "we were cutting the silence of the sea" (*íbamos cortando el silencio del mar*). (III.145) The shadows are, therefore, identified as human. But the reader is, at first, less affected by the association of humans and shadows than by the combination of shadows and silence. The two words place us in a singularly

black-and-white world, with a feeling of foreboding. In the same
stanza, a reference to fish that make isochronous jumps is reinforced by the adverb "rhythmically" (*acompasadamente*), (III.
145) and this image adds to the feeling of shadow and silence
an element of periodicity, of counting off. This impression ultimately evolves into an appreciation of the passage of time.

The poem is developed with a minimal number of finite verbs
—they are not used in the basic imagery, but to specify some
action in the midst of the imagery. At the beginning of the second
stanza, the repetition in "Sailing, sailing" (*Bogar, bogar*), (III.
145) creates a feeling of duration that contrasts with the sequential "leaps" (*saltos*), (III.145) that end the first stanza.
After accepting this feeling of duration, we feel darkness and
the loss of direction in imagery that suggests inexpressible suffering. The destinationless journey continues in the third stanza.
There is neither dawn nor horizon. But there is a swish in the
water and "something falls and disappears in the deep night"
(*algo cae y en la noche profunda desaparece*). (III.145) Now
we have a strong feeling of loss and of the inability to recover
whatever has disappeared. This reaction ultimately becomes a
reference to the lost beloved.

Stanza four begins with a reference to the presence of fear
among the shadows; they are so afraid indeed that, in spite of
the sense of loss, they ask no questions. By this time, the shadows
have become quite human, and at this point we have a feeling
of endurance; but it is not a feeling of heroic endurance, because
our reaction is pity rather than admiration. At the same moment,
the sea takes on a quality of "monotonous harmony" (*monótona
armonía*), (III.145) and communicates a feeling of stability that
finally turns into the passage through life without concerned
reaction. The moon, which might give, through its light, a more
meaningful life—a life of knowing—is absent.

The fifth stanza begins with a repetition of the "sailing, sailing"
of the second stanza, and with the same sense of duration. The
silence of the crew reinforces the stolid acceptance of the inevitable and also underlines the state of ignorance that silence
suggests throughout the poem. In a question, the poet indicates
that origin and destination are equally unknown. Still we keep
going, "insomnia in our anguished eyes" (*insomnia en las pupilas
angustiadas*), (III.146) and Death is at the helm.

Neither the words nor the intensity of "Ballad of the Living Dead ("Romance del muerto vivo") can be appreciated fully without recalling that the year of the publication of *Roses in the Amphora* was also the year of the death of Enrique González Rojo, the poet son. Although we cannot be sure whether some of the poems were written before or after this second tragic departure, the reference to "where *he* and *she* went" (*a donde ella y él se fueron*), (III.154)—the emphasis is the poet's— indicates that "Ballad of the Living Dead" was written after; and the almost anesthetized state of the author in this poem bears a great similarity to the pitiful endurance in "Phantom Ship." In "Ballad . . .," EGM is trying, in the midst of over- whelming sorrow, to distinguish reality. In the first of its three stanzas, the poet imagines that he too is dead and is looking for the ones he has lost. A feeling approaching panic grips us as he looks for them and cannot find them, as he gropes in hopeless darkness, imagining "that I am a shadow among shadows in an endless night" (*que soy sombra entre sombras en una noche sin término*). (III.154)

Life returns in the second stanza, and there is a soul so much a part of him that to separate himself from it would be like tearing out his own soul. The feeling here is that the poet is as he was before, but in a strangely limited way: the feeling of being alive is contrary to his actual state, so he perceives this life as if he were dreaming that he is awake. He has no sure hold on reality, either in the state of the first stanza, or in the state of the second. The third stanza is addressed to the beloved, and identifies her in a most revealing way: "you through whom the night sings/ and the silence is illuminated" (*tú por quien la noche canta/ y se ilumina el silencio*). (III.155) These beautiful lines are very close to the definition of communion with all things that the poet wrote many years before in "You Will Pass Over the Life of Things." We now have a sense of the beloved as a means of communication with the wholeness of the universe. And the feeling of knowing through the beloved is stated definitively when the poet says "only you can tell me/ if I am alive or I am dead" (*solo tú podrás decirme/ si estoy vivo o estoy muerto*). (III.155)

"The Yoke" ("La yunta") is more analytical and considers the meaning of the collaboration of love and suffering. The sonnet's sextet makes a fine contrast in the poet's wondering. If love is suffering, why does he insist on loving more? Still, if love is gentle, why does he insist on suffering? The poem does not attempt to resolve the question. It is part of the poet's attempt to work out an understanding of his present condition.

A similar analysis is seen in another sonnet, "Presence of Sorrow" ("Presencia del dolor"), but in this case the poet creates a deeper feeling. Speaking to sorrow personified, the poet states his question in the first line: "Tell me what more you want than to be present" (*Dime qué quieres más que estar presente*"). (III.144) We sense impatience on the part of the poet who feels that sorrow, more than simply controlling his emotion, plays an active role in his existence. He describes sorrow as a "goad" (*aguijón*) (III.144); and since it pervades both place and time, it is inescapable. It is the goad that puzzles the poet. The sonnet's octave suggests that he is quite willing to accept sorrow's presence, but does not understand the quality of sorrow that insists on an active role, that makes him go outside himself. In the sextet, he begs sorrow to enlarge the wound, but to stay hidden inside.

"Evening Miracle" ("Milagro de la tarde") is closely related to "Presence of Sorrow" because the poet feels the impulse to sing in spite of his grief. He is tired of activity, but not of contemplation. Then as he shrinks within himself, a song breaks the silence, and the poet answers. In the last stanza we are made to feel that he has captured again the moment of knowing the relationship between silent contemplation and the journey toward knowing. When he speaks of the double miracle of the song and "the imprint of the star on the road" (*la huella de la estrella en el camino*"), (III.143) we relate the image to the first quatrain where he expresses fatigue from the footprint on the road (here we may understand the active quest of communion), but says that he is not tired of observing the star (quiet contemplation). The two are joined in the final image.

The gay fatalism of "Wings of Wax" ("Alas de cera") suggests the possibility that it was written before the death of the beloved. To a limited extent, we do feel the process of the poet working his way through to understanding; but the general feeling varies considerably from the poems of this collection. This sonnet is certainly an anticipation of death, but from a greater distance than in the other poems. What is more important, the death involves both, not one. There is a clear relationship between loving and the poetic quest, and the image of the ascent is predominant. It is, of course, when the ascent takes them too close to the sun that they will plummet downward, but together.

"August Madrigal" ("Madrigal de agosto") is a more meaningful poem in which we experience the joy of a moment of reunion with the beloved. The basis of the poem is a dream in which the beloved appears as a source of renewal. In his agony, the poet spoke her name. The second stanza moves from dream to reality, but without losing the miracle of the dream completely.

> I opened my eyes, and I thought it is certain
> that I live by your shadow and that you are mine . . .
> If I blessed your love while I was sleeping,
> I bless it more now that I am awake!
>
> *(Abrí los ojos, y pensé que es cierto*
> *que vivo de tu sombra y que eres mía . . .*
> *¡Si bendije tu amor mientras dormía,*
> *más lo bendigo ahora, ya despierto!)* (III.153)

The calm joy of "August Madrigal" is very different from the anguish of "The Yoke." The beneficent act of the beloved is also apparent in "Peace" ("Paz"), a sonnet in which she is the source of comfort, peace, serenity. The imagery of the octave communicates this feeling of salvation from anguish. The first tercet recognizes the act as of the past, but in the second tercet we feel the poet's ability to retain the benefits of the gift and to look forward to a renewal. Both "Peace" and "August Madrigal" produce something approaching an awareness of the beloved's continued presence. "Berceuse" develops this feeling even more strongly.

> Sleep in me as in a secure place;
> consider that there is a life within each dream,
> and in love's present forget
> yesterday's betrayal and the future's shadow.
>
> *(Duérmete en mí como en lugar seguro;*
> *piensa que en cada sueño hay una vida,*
> *y en el presente del amor olvida*
> *traición de ayer y sombra del futuro.)* (III.156)

The second quatrain develops the gentle protectiveness that we find in the first. The sextet produces the feeling of union of poet and beloved, and of her reawakening at the sound of his "new song" (*"nueva canción"*). (III.156)

IV Under the Mortal Sign

It is not easy to speak of the poet's grief following the death of his poet son. The fact of this second separation within the space of a few years is difficult enough. But there is an almost unbearable poignancy in the death of the poet son of a poet father. We feel strongly inclined to leave it reverently untouched. Still, the poet's sorrow is a shared sorrow, and we enter the work to participate in the creative act. We deceive ourselves if we intend to discover how González Martínez reacted to the death of his son; our concern can only be the relationship between the continuity of life and the continuity of the poetic search. And what we do comprehend of this relationship, we discover not in the form of an objective resolution, but in the process of creating the poem.

Under the Mortal Sign (*Bajo el signo mortal*) was published in 1942. Some of the poems carry dates of composition, and the first poem of the volume, "The Dead Son" ("El hijo muerto"), is dated May 9, 1939, the date of the death of Enrique González Rojo. It is a poem of sorrow and wondering, and we see again the nearly anesthetized state of the poet struck by inexplicable loss—almost a repetition of the wounded astonishment that sets the tone of some of the poems written after the loss of the beloved. We feel the immediate reaction of desperation and the will to retain something of the departed—the memory of how he looked. Then there is a burst of the sense of relationship that communicates not only love, but the feeling of the course of life and a dependency on the son's youth. The feeling is interrupted by the inevitable and unanswerable question of the cause of the tragedy. After that we enter into the feeling of lost continuity, of a logical order gone awry, of a hope denied. The image of the poetic touch appears here as it did in "Victory Over Time," the poem in which EGM first expressed the hope of poetic continuity in his son. The poem ends with interrogation, the poet asking against whom can he rebel, or with whom can he plead.

The third volume of the "Polis" edition of EGM's collected poems carries this dedication:

I dedicate this volume to the clear memory of my son Enrique, who died in the flower of poetry on the ninth day of May, 1939.

(Dedico este volumen a la clara memoria de mi hijo Enrique, muerto en flor de poesía el día nueve de mayo de 1939.)

On the following page, separate from the text, appears "Last Journey" ("Ultimo viaje"), one of the author's most beautiful poems. The desperation of "The Dead Son" has disappeared; we now feel the hope that the questions may eventually be answered. What remains is a feeling of temporary loneliness and the expectation of reunion that will bring with it the answer to the eternal riddle. The first stanza communicates the feeling of loss, of the voice now silent.

> He has gone the way
> of silence. He goes before
> me. He carries his torch
> safe now from the air's treachery.
>
> (*Camino del silencio*
> *se ha ido. Va delante*
> *de mí. Lleva su antorcha*
> *a salvo ya de la traición del aire.*)[5]

We feel here the studied calm of the poet, reducing the event to its minimum. The short, almost abrupt sentences suggest incipient weeping, as the poet faces the fact of separation. But even the last sentence of this stanza brings an expansion of the poet's ability to speak, and continues with growing awareness of the circumstance into the next stanza:

> He goes whispering the verse he could not
> speak that last evening.
> His smile vanished, and in his eyes
> trembles the deep fear of one who *now knows*.
>
> (*Va musitando el verso que no pudo*
> *decir la última tarde.*
> *Se perdió la sonrisa, y en sus ojos*
> *tiembla el hondo pavor del que ya sabe.*)

So we experience the moment of the departure, and with it the loss of poetic continuity. The third stanza combines the search for the departed and the agonizing memory of the filial relationship, now lost. Then in the fourth stanza we feel the expectation of reunion, and the relationship reestablished.

> When my footsteps, hastened by absence
> and following behind him, catch up,
> the two of us together before the glass that melds
> images freed from time,
> I will see his face and I will watch his forehead
> fall upon my paternal shoulder.

(Cuando mis pasos, que la auscencia anima
y le siguen en pos, le den alcance,
juntos los dos ante el cristal que funde
liberadas del tiempo las imágenes,
veré su faz y miraré su frente
en el hombro paterno desmayarse.)

Throughout the poem, the author's sentences have become longer, their structure more complicated, as he has moved from the minimal, worldly realization of tragedy and loss toward an awareness of a fuller reality that can be expressed only in terms of expectation. The growing feeling of hope reaches climax in the certainty of the last two lines, an exquisite anticipation:

> There we will both learn who orders
> a day of leaving, and the journey's reason.

> *(Allí sabremos ambos quién ordena*
> *partir un día, y la razón del viaje.)*

González Martínez continues the process of working through to an acceptance of his personal loss and an understanding of his own anticipation of death. He is patiently at his task in "Alleluia to Death" ("Aleluya de la muerte"), in which he translates an unsatisfactorily rational proposition into poetic expectation. The poem is long, divided into four parts, and is written in a traditional stanza of six lines and rhymed. The regularity of the poem lends it a certain intellectual dignity. It is different from the formal beauty of a sonnet; rather, it suggests an extended contemplation. The first part anticipates an expansion of life through the introduction of an unknown dimension. And we feel in the first stanza a relationship of death and life that is almost subliminal in quality. But the relationship develops in the rest of the poem. Within this expanded life, much of the communication that EGM has sought will be realized.

The second part of the poem is anticipation of reunion with the poet's loved ones. In the third part, the life-death enigma becomes a question, and the poet wonders why death attracts him even when he is not tired of living. He uses the analogy of a tree whose roots become stronger as the tree reaches up. The fourth part moves through the poet's disappointment for not having found complete communion with the universe, and toward the expectation of fulfillment.

In "Prayer to Life" ("Plegaria a la vida"), the poet has reached a position of resignation. He is neither afraid to die nor does he seek death. It is another step in the process of working through to a valid position confronting the future. These steps in the process should not be taken, however, to mean a steady progress toward a state of enlightenment. The intensity of the moments varies considerably, and even the basic characteristics of the emotions vary. Often we feel the tendency to withdraw and wait, but we also feel the impulse to reach out and seek. Sometimes what the poet seeks appears to be unobtainable and at other times it seems to be almost within reach. There are times when we feel keenly the failure of the poet to achieve any kind of fulfillment, but at others we know there has been a deep communication that will be even deeper in the future.

Under the Mortal Sign is divided into several sections. The title section is followed by a group of poems under the title of "The Gentle Wound" ("La dulce herida"). These are love poems, and their best moments are when they capture the feeling of the beloved's continued presence.

The element of time in "The Meeting" ("El encuentro") can function on either of two levels: it can be understood as the first meeting of poet and beloved, or it can be projected into a reunion after the beloved's departure. We know from the first of its ten short lines that the reality of the circumstance is not reality in the usual sense:

> We were wandering aimlessly
> on the wings of I know not what;
>
> *(Vagábamos sin sentido*
> *en alas de un no sé qué;)* (*Bajo el signo mortal.* 35)

Within the poem, he recovers what he had lost, she captures what she had anticipated. From this meeting we have the feeling of reunion. We discover in subsequent poems that the poet has discovered the reality of the beloved's continued presence, and it is this truth that makes these poems more than a mere statement of grief.

Nowhere is her presence more vivid than in "Week-end,"[6] perhaps because the first stanza shows the persistence of the poet's awareness of her in contrast to the weakness of an attempt to make her absence a reality.

This minimal flight that strives
to change your presence into distance,
makes me feel you are all the more mine
and, the more absent you are, the closer you come.

*(Esta mínima fuga que se afana
por cambiar tu presencia en lejanía,
me hace sentirte cada vez mía
y, cuanto más ausente, más cercana.)* (44)

The paradoxical reality is continued into the second stanza, where the poet wonders why he cannot see her if she is present, how she can be with him if she is far away. But there is no doubt that she is near, because she is a source of renewal. Transcending the limits of objective reality in the third stanza, we are assured of her presence. Faced with solitude and presence in the fourth stanza, the poet resolves the paradox in the last two lines:

Time and distance are fictions,
and absence and forgetting, phantoms.

*(Ficciones son el tiempo y la distancia,
y fantasmas la ausencia y el olvido.)* (44)

V Second Awakening and Other Poems

The title poem of *Second Awakening* (*Segundo Despertar*), 1945, indicates that the poetry of this volume is a continuation of EGM's process of working through. We are witnessing not the experience of a second awakening already accomplished, but the anticipation of how that awakening will be, when it comes. The future tense projects us into this feeling of anticipation. In non-poetic language we have to say, rather weakly, that what the poet expects is fulfillment: "I will follow my course to the exalted possession of what is mine" (*seguiré mi rumbo a la alta posesión de lo que es mío*). (*Segundo despertar.* IX) The poem is a series of thirteen quatrains that look forward exultantly to what the poet can expect. The high point comes in the last stanza when the "prelude that I carry in my soul . . . will be a song" (*preludio que en el alma llevo . . . será canción*). (XII)

"Nascent Soul" ("Alma naciente") creates not only the expectancy of any state of beginning, but also combines with that feeling an awareness of absolute innocence. It is a state of being pure life. As he has done in other similar moments, EGM makes extensive use of the infinitive form here, thereby avoiding contamination of the purity of the emotion by suggestion of human limitation. The resulting emphasis is on being on the brink of being. The anticipation of newness is sustained throughout the poem in a series of images that communicate a sense of beginning. The suggestion of a state which will be envied by bird and rose transports us to a condition on the other side of EGM's fundamental poetic search. It has been the poet who envied bird and rose, who sometimes felt not only the desire to communicate with them, but to be them. The anticipated condition turns the quest inside out.

In "Ballad of the Tree" ("Balada del árbol"), EGM restores the activity of life to the attitude of expectation. He uses the image of the tree to symbolize his poetic process, or in a more general sense, his life process during the period of anticipation. The first of the poem's seven tercets establishes the fact that this "tree which is rooted in death" (*árbol con raíz de muerte*), (XIII) grows higher and stronger. In the next two stanzas (the past tense is used here) the poet says that the tree was nourished by his sorrow; then changing to the present tense within the third stanza, weeping turns to song. It is at this point that we begin to feel the creative use of sorrow. The fourth tercet increases the feeling of productivity. Then the fifth takes a contemplative turn and the poet finds it remarkable that death was the source of this creativeness. The tree even softens the bitter memory of its beginning, in the sixth stanza: "Petals of snow carpet/ the tomb where you were born" (*Pétalos de nieve alfombran la tumba donde naciste*). (XIV) In the same tercet the poet communicates a very strong feeling of the creation of the tree by death when he says "in every crevice that you opened/ voices of absence name you" (*en cada grieta que abriste/ voces de ausencia te nombran*). (XIV) The feeling here is not one of creation that goes on endlessly. The naming of the tree by the voices of absence is a constant gift of life from those who have departed. The final tercet emphasizes the actuality of life, of the continued process of living. There is a certain kind of resignation in this stanza which has developed throughout the poem—an active resignation that recognizes the creative power of what we call death, and finds within that recognition a way of living toward death itself.

The poet causes our intuition to function along with his own, and that is the way we face reality in "Ballad of the Tree." But the poet does not dedicate his expression completely to intuition. "To an Absent Soul" ("A un alma ausente") combines the intuitive reach within rational questioning. EGM begins with a three-lined stanza that communicates the perfect union of poet and beloved, the condition in which the act of one is not complete without the act of the other.

> Because you knew what I never said
> and now will never say, I weep for my
> own death in yours, and bury myself in life.

> *(Porque sabías lo que nunca dije*
> *y no diré ya más, lloro en tu muerte*
> *mi propia muerte, y me sepulto en vida.) (XV)*

In the second stanza we have the feeling of the poet actively making the transition from this worldly life to an infinite state of reunion and timelessness. The third stanza anticipates specifically the reunion of the poet's loved ones, and generally of all men, in a kind of amorphous body. All "will go to the same sea" (*irán al mismo mar*). (XV) Then in the following stanza we share the poet's reluctance to accept this lack of identity, and he wonders if the particularity of life as we know it—"this small and vacillating life" (*esta vida pequeña y vacilante*), (XVI)—is never to return. We feel the loss of the creative impulse in the possibility of losing particularity. Even though this life of particularity appears in the last stanza as a life of eternal questioning, we feel the need to sustain the quest, as if the answer might mark the end of what we wish to retain. Right at the end of the poem, we are very much within this small and vacillating life, asking the beloved for an answer to the question.

In a series of three sonnets, "Triptych of the Journey" ("Tríptico del viaje"), EGM captures three moments related to the beloved. The first begins with an awareness of her departure, moves to a feeling of alternating joy and grief, and ends in the poet's acute awareness of living. We feel the continued presence of the beloved and a considerable joy. The second sonnet uses the tree symbol to communicate the dual action of reaching up and holding on at the same time. The sound of bees introduces the awareness of the need of love. The intensity of loving continues into the third sonnet, but the mood changes now to the sense of loss which is evoked by the awareness of impending death. The three moments combine to form a story of poet and beloved. Her continued presence is even more strongly felt in "Suspension" ("Suspensión"), a carefully wrought sonnet where the poet, in his spiritual ascent, is joined by the beloved in a union that is as certain as their wedding. But the new union has the combined and paradoxical quality of absence and presence at once.

> In a strange suspension, the flight upward
> kept on its course without leaving the ground,
> the present and the distant joined as one.

> *(En rara suspensión, el alto vuelo*
> *siguió su rumbo sin dejar el suelo,*
> *fundidos lo presente y lo lejano.)* (XLII)

"The Track" ("El rastro") is a pair of quatrains in which the first observes and the second questions, recalling a method of composition that EGM used in some of the poetry of the 1920's. Here he uses the procedure to pose a question about the nature of death and, by implication, what happens afterward. He ponders footsteps that disappear unexpectedly. The question is whether their maker was swallowed by an abyss, or just as suddenly grew wings and ascended. We know that the poet's attitude toward the final question is one that does not really anticipate a positive answer, though intuition takes us very close to it at times. Certainly EGM, proceeding rationally from a rational position, does not attach himself to any specific faith, but frequently and sometimes agonizingly, searches for a deeper truth. This search is felt in "Sacred Fire" ("Fuego sagrado"). It is a plea to the beloved to maintain the sacred fire, which does not refer to any religion, but to the sense of the sacred. The feeling is very similar to that of many poems that communicate the profound sense of life. The journey toward the answer, toward knowing, toward communion, toward reunion, is given form by the impulse that sends us onward. In "Sacred Fire" the poet assumes that if the fire is not tended, "we will be mad birds that go from branch to branch/ without remembering the rhythm of their old song" (*seremos aves locas que van de rama en rama/ sin recordar el ritmo de su vieja canción*). (XXIV)

The poet himself is not always certain that the sacred fire is tended. His position between abyss and heights causes him to feel, in "Naked Soul" ("Alma desnuda"), that he might have done better, might have seen life in a different way. Here we feel that the poet is confessing that he might have been more creative, and the doubt transfers easily to the reader who enters into the confession with the author. EGM knows perfectly well that in this moment of self-revelation, there is no point in talking about redoing the past. He must live in his middle position: "Between heights and abyss I sustain myself" (*entre altura y abismo me sostengo*; (XLV) and we feel within the poem that man can hardly expect anything better. What is not felt keenly in this poem, though EGM does communicate it in other places, is the creative synthesis of the movement between heights and abyss. Here the mood is more similar to "Interrogation" ("Interrogaciones"), where the poet wonders if the rhythmic vacillation is indeed life. The meaning of the poem reaches us primarily because it is a series of questions, only questions, and they emphasize the lack of positive progress.

"Pleasure in Uncertainty" ("Placer de incertidumbre"), if it were read carelessly and outside the context of this volume, might indicate that the poet has come to terms with the inevitable and has talked himself into a state of euphoric passivity. There is, in fact, a kind of resignation in this poem, but it is anything but passive. It is an expression of the living that goes on between the heights and abyss of "Naked Soul": "I ceaselessly interrogate my destiny/ and I take pleasure in its silence" (*Interrogo sin tregua a mi destino/ y gozo en su callar*). (XLIX) But the poet is not withdrawn from life; rather, he rejoices in it—through feeling rather than through knowing. This is the state of being pure emotion. The two quatrains communicate the feeling in a parable-like fashion. And we feel the intensity of living without uncertainty. The condition, however, is a very temporary one, because the second tercet expresses the expectation that death will remove uncertainty and yearning.

Whatever the promise of death, several poems reinforce the reluctance to give up this "small and vacillating life." "Soul Adrift" ("Alma sin rumbo") asks the soul when the new life will come to pass, and what the announcement will be like. These questions are in the first three of fifteen stanzas. Then we feel again the creative use of sorrow which has acted as a sort of expiation in the poet's life: "Sorrow that purifies/ the blackest conscience, has touched me" (*Dolor, que vuelve pura/ la más negra conciencia, me ha tocado*). (LIII) The desire to combine in some fashion the present and the future develops through to the end of the poem: "May what dies and what endures ascend in a pure flame" (*en una llama pura/asciendan lo que muere y lo que dura*). (LVI) This concept also carries out the feeling of the tenth stanza where the poet hopes for a union of past and present, with the feeling developed by the use of the image of dawn joining sunset. The position from which he projects his hopes is the suspension between heights and abyss that we have seen in other poems.

"The Poet and His Shadow" ("El poeta y su sombra") communicates the feeling of identification with the world, completely and without shadow. Then, when the time comes for him to be shadow, he will be that and nothing more. EGM's imagery is excellent. We see him in a sun-drenched world, observing his shadow, and we feel that permanence is within the poet and that the shadow is ephemeral, "a useless present." (LVII) The clarity of the present can be clarity only if it is shadowless; but at the time when shadow becomes the norm, then the new circumstance will have its own clarity because the poet will become shadow within shadow, and there will be no conflict to obscure the knowledge that comes with perfect union.

VI Thistle in the Wind

In spite of his state of uncertainty, EGM frequently perceives life as a pleasant experience; but even when it is not pleasant, there is no doubt that it is indeed life—active, not an unproductive waiting. Just as the creativity of "Pleasure in Uncertainty" is an act of living toward death, the title poem of *Thistle in the Wind* (*Vilano al viento*), 1948, is an affirmation of life, stated in a more somber mood. Here the past rushes up to meet the present, and the poet wonders who, what, and where he is. He walks in shadow, and as the long trajectory of his poetic search concentrates now in the reality of a single moment, he wonders what it is that has made him want to know. But the fact is that he still does seek the answer; and though he proceeds blindly, he does so in the never-ending quest: "I walk gropingly . . . But my own hand/ struggles and pulls to remove the blindfold" (*A tientas voy . . . Pero mi propia mano/ pugna y se crispa por rasgar la venda*). (*Vilano al viento*. 12) He sings during the journey, hoping that the song will find a response.

It is this erratic song that EGM compares to the pollen scattered by a thistle in the wind.

"The Incomplete Message" ("El mensaje incompleto") is a retrospective poem where EGM builds carefully to his present state of feeling that he has not completed his poetic message. The poem begins with a statement of the condition—"I had something more to say in life" (*Yo tenía más que decir en la vida*), (49)—as a proposition, and ends with the same statement, the problem still unresolved. The best of the poem is the recapitulation of the poetic quest. In the five intermediate quatrains we feel again a large part of the joyful expectation that we felt in the earlier poetry, especially *The Hidden Paths*.

"The Incomplete Message" is not a poem of frustration. It does not communicate a sense of failure, because the poet is aware of what he was able to do as well as of what he did not accomplish. When he says "I wanted the invisible, in rare communion/ to converse with me" (*Quise que lo invisible, en comunión extraña/ dialogara conmigo*), (49), we know that the wish was only partially granted; but we also recall the resplendent moments of knowing, when he says "I found life complete in terror of night/ and in the blood laugh of an open pomegranate" (*hallé la vida íntegra en el pavor nocturno/ y en la risa de sangre de una granada abierta*). (49) The sense is not of frustration, but of incompleteness—the inevitable incompleteness of the valid poetic quest. The awareness of it makes it hard for EGM to round out the recall of his experience. His own poetic integrity, of course, would not allow him to complete the circle.

Existence on the creative edge of life is far from comfortable. Luisa Luisi, the Argentine critic, in a comparison of EGM and Amado Nervo, points out that Nervo's trajectory ended in the peace and consolation of a definite religion, after he had experienced most of the major religions and philosophies of the world; EGM maintained his doubt and the open quest, and Luisi thinks that "there is more greatness, more intimate suffering, more painful courage, in the struggle that does not end" (*hay más grandeza, más sufrimiento íntimo, más dolorosa fortaleza, en la lucha que no termina*).[7] There is not the slightest doubt that EGM's poetry proves Luisi's point. We must remember, however, the paradoxical appearance of the continued quest: it must seek its own end, or it is not a quest at all. Yet, if the goal is reached, the quest comes to an end. The poet's mood necessarily varies.

"Last Sea" ("Ultimo mar") creates the moment of ambivalence when the poet would like to remove uncertainty and maintain the search. Even here, it is clear that the certainty could come late.

> I journey among shadows . . . But I should like
> before the word becomes mute
> and the eye sightless, to nail my doubt
> on the timbers of some cross.
>
> *(Viajo entre sombras . . . Pero yo quisiera,*
> *antes que la palabra quede muda*
> *y el ojo sin visión clavar mi duda*
> *sobre las tablas de una cruz cualquiera.)* (77)

This stanza is the first in a poem where the desire for certainty is permeated by the impulse to continue the search.

"Insatiable Longing" ("El anhelo insaciable") contributes greatly to rounding EGM's poetic circle, not in the sense of resolving the paradox of the quest, but in communicating the persistence of the poet's longing. It has much the same feeling as "You Will Pass Over the Life of Things" and similar poems of earlier years. "Insatiable Longing" consists of seven quatrains. Each of the first four begins with "I should like" (*Quisiera*), and expresses the desire of experiences that might be described as initial or fundamental or virginal: "the first emotion of a reflection of sun on the plain (*la emoción primera de un reflejo de sol en la pradera*), "the naked soul before a mirror" (*el alma desnuda ante el espejo*). (179) The imagery of these stanzas invites the reader to participate in the creation of circumstances of purity, silence, freshness, introspection. Then, the creative power of the poem becomes even more intense in the last three stanzas when the poet drops the "I should like" and begins with the infinitive. The change enhances the actuality of the act created within the poem. The feeling is that of living life purely as life, to feel more than to know, and finally

> to join the rhythm of the universe
> with my heart, beat to beat,
> and to bequeath what I have dreamed and lived
> in the melodic eternity of a poem.

(unir el palpitar del universo
al corazón, latido con latido,
y legar lo soñado y lo vivido
en la sonora eternidad de un verso.) (180)

EGM's concern for the song that he will leave behind makes
"Eulogy to the Sonnet" ("Elogio del soneto") particularly rele-
vant to the poetry written as he is closing his circle. This is
the only time that he mentions the formal side of the creative
process. His words of praise are not surprising since many of
EGM's best poems are in sonnet form, and it is probable that,
at this time, he felt that they would be most enduring. This
sonnet itself is a very good one in which a stream of images
produces a feeling of restraint and, finally, of fulfillment.

The poet's sense of sorrow has not left him. It is still a goad
that will neither be silent within him, nor will it be truly pro-
ductive. "That Sorrow" ("Aquel dolor") uses the image of a
dammed-up stream to express the feeling. It could be relieved
if an outlet were found that would allow the water to communicate with the earth; but that is impossible, at least at this
moment when sorrow is not creative. It runs constantly, but
finds no outlet.

The poet's suspended state between abyss and heights reaches
a climax in "The Pendulum" ("El péndulo"). The uncertainty
in which the poet finds himself is the same as in "Pleasure in
Uncertainty," but the emotion evoked is entirely different. What
we feel in "The Pendulum" is impatience. More graphically and
more accurately described, the feeling is one of being submitted
to a rhythmic torture. The pendulum moves in each stanza and
thus there is a constant swinging from the extreme of the abyss
to the extreme of the heights. At the end, there is an almost
petulant burst of let's-have-done-with-it impatience. It matters
not to the poet whether he burns his wings in ascent or loses
his footing and slips into the abyss.

In the unrest that incites me,
I only pursue, good or bad,
the emotion of a new life!

(¡En la inquietud que me subleva,
sólo persigo, buena o mala,
la emoción de una vida nueva!) (38)

We must be careful to read "The Pendulum" as poetry, not as philosophy. Only the pitifully misguided would read this poem as a statement of principle; what it really is can be discovered only by creating with the poet this tortured moment—a part of his reality.

An entirely different mood is developed in "The Waiting" ("La espera"). Here we feel the calmness of the man who neither seeks nor avoids death. He recognizes the difference between the one who faces death with faith and the one who faces it with doubt. But even this difference is not disturbing: "One confides; but the other waits" (*Uno confía; mas el otro espera*). (111) The strength of this line does not come through well in English, because Spanish *espera* communicates "expectation" or "hope" as much as it does "waiting." The line, in Spanish, shows the contrast between the passivity of one who feels secure and the excitement of the endless search. And in another stanza, the dreamer welcomes the arrival of death "as the azure prolongation of the dream" (*como la azul prolongación del sueño*). (109)

"Octave of the Broken Thread" ("Octava del hilo roto") synthesizes much of the poet's vacillation. It is an excellent poem, very *conceptista*, a little sad, a little funny, very sly, and completely appealing. The reader is not in exact identification with the poet, but rather has the feeling that EGM is taking the reader into his confidence. The poet identifies his condition as one that has existed for some time: he wanders about a garden in which he is imprisoned and is peaceful. The description of the garden as "delight, labyrinth, and torture" (*deleite, laberinto y tortura*), (115) covers the gamut of his response to his condition.

An Ariadne lends him a thread by which he can find his way to the exit. (The present tense is maintained and we feel all the more keenly the poet's reaction.) But the poet has turned his prison into a refuge, and breaks the string because he does not want to leave.

> and I spend my hours, with hidden malice,
> in pretended search of the enigmatic door.

> (*y me paso las horas, con malicia encubierta,*
> *en la busca fingida de enigmática puerta.*) (115)

VII   The New Narcissus and Other Poems

The New Narcissus (*El Nuevo Narciso*), 1952, is the last
volume planned by EGM and was published the year of his
death. Its title poem is less lyric, more abrupt than is usual in
the poetry of his later years. The composition creates a sense
of striving to find the most appropriate image within the very
making of the poem. Its communication is again the eternal
searching. We have the feeling of reaching toward the answer
hidden among many directions that the search might take. But
even within this clouded view, we feel a certain serenity in
knowing that the answer exists, durable, imperturbable, even
if the question is not asked.

Approximately one fourth of this small collection is a series
of "Stanzas" ("Estancias"), twenty-one octaves and a concluding
sonnet.[8] These poems fill EGM's devoted reader—and there is
no doubt that EGM's reader is intimately related to the poet—
with a wonderful feeling of calm. Here is the comprehension
of his circumstance that is the best that we could desire for the
poet or for ourselves. The poet's reconciliation, which is seen
in different perspectives throughout the series, is apparent in
the simple recognition of his state, in the first stanza. Although
the poet does not see the vision clearly, he has not lost the
remembered vision of the journey, and he waits, singing. Then
he expresses his feeling of being very much a part of the world
of others.

> I am of the chorus; neither new resonance
> nor rare timbre of initial message;
> I am enchanted by the eternal melody
> that, for belonging to all, is the more mine.

> *(Del coro soy; ni resonancia nueva*
> *ni raro timbre de inicial mensaje;*
> *me seduce la eterna melodía*
> *que, por ser la de todos, es más mía.)* (10)

The poet is aware of his particularity both before and after
the present state, but for this moment, he joins with the rest.
In the second stanza, the intensity of living comes into focus.
And life—that is, the pure act of living—is what matters. The
qualifying aspects of life—joy, sorrow, success, failure—are of
minor importance. What endures is the will to live.

Later we feel the dignity with which the poet awaits death, his continued openness to all that is about him, his calm interrogation regarding the source of the final decisions. The twelfth stanza has a strong feeling of movement forward in the direction of the future accepted. Even though we understand the poet's self-professed ignorance of himself as he remains suspended between abyss and heights, we sense his reaching out.

In the fifteenth, EGM reiterates his relationship with men which is expressed in the first stanza; but here it is the need of sharing their agony which, as in the case of the eternal melody, is more the poet's for being the agony of all. Then recalling his particular sorrow, we feel as we have in other poems, that he does not consider himself betrayed by life. Rather, sorrow added a dimension to his quest. From this point, the stanzas build through the redemptive act of poetry and toward the new life. The sonnet that concludes the series uses nature imagery to move us from the feeling of the old and wasted, of being essentially dead, to a hopeful anticipation that is clearly life.

"Bedazzled Joy" ("El gozo alucinado") is one of EGM's most creative poems. It would probably be appropriate, in this case, to understand in *alucinado* some of the feeling of madness that we find in its English cognate "hallucinated." The first two quatrains communicate the poet's incorporation of everything into himself with a certainty that makes him master of them all. The reality that he dominates is made up of intangibles. Color becomes a part of him, but he does not paint it; he contains sound; the tree is the essence of the tree (*aliento*) rather than its greenness, and it is the essence that the poet commands. In the third stanza he informs us, "I model worlds in order to make them mine" (*modelo mundos para hacerlos míos*). (18)

The poet continues his journey over the life of things for six more quatrains. His perception is always of what is essential rather than of what is obvious. He retains not the vision of the dropping of water, but the message that he heard in it. His experiences of communication come back, concentrated in a moment, and finally the sense of reunion is complete: "the eternal rhythm of the world fills my hours and I feel it mine" (*el eterno palpitar del mundo llena mis horas y lo siento mío*). (19)

In "Double Task" ("Doble tarea"), EGM creates a sense of quiet and intense passing of time, and the calmness of living during the period of waiting. The double task is, of course, the anticipation of death and the maintaining of hope. The task becomes a single one because the two aspects of existence join to constitute an active living toward death. The poem does in fact join them within the poem, by alternate reference in odd and even lines of the first stanza, and then by assuming them as the integrated characteristic of the waiting period, in the second stanza.

"Posthumous Image" ("Imagen póstuma") shows how far the poet's anticipation, and reconciliation, could project him into the future. Here the poet feels himself apart from himself as he is, contemplating his persistence in the world, and still questioning.

> I am my own shadow set loose;
> the body is hidden, but the shadow remains,
> and crosses life in spectral flight
> like a fleeting form that mimics well
> the line and gesture of the image gone.

> *(Yo soy mi propia sombra desasida;*
> *se esconde el cuerpo, mas la sombra queda,*
> *y en un vuelo espectral cruza la vida*
> *como forma flotante que remeda*
> *contorno y gesto de la imagen ida.)* (19)

The poet asks who would obscure or destroy the image. Faithful to himself, he must always question, whatever the perspective in which he views his own reality, must always envision the possibility of the journey's perfect end, must always maintain himself on the creative edge.

CHAPTER 5

The Prophetic Commitment

I looked at the earth
and its agony came to
me more deeply—*Babel*

I The Flood of Fire

FOR the first time, we approach EGM's poetry out of chronological order. The purpose is to place together three longer poems, all concerned with the fate of the world of men. They are indeed related to the poet's long and ardent search for profound truth, but they have a special meaning because of what we may call their social commitment. We have often seen, in EGM's poetry, an anguished struggle between two opposing motivations; on the one hand, a desire to follow the road to clarity through deeply intimate, poetic experience, and on the other hand, a certain feeling of obligation to the human muddle that is too short-sighted to see what is perfectly obvious to those who wish to see. At times the poet has shown impatience toward the insensitive human mass. At other times his reaction has been closer to pity. There have been times when he has felt a Baudelairean despair over the role of the poet. Whatever the reaction, he has always been aware of the difference between those who see and those who do not. Perhaps we might truthfully say that he was tragically aware.

The first of the long poems is *The Flood of Fire* (*El diluvio de fuego*) which was published in 1938, the year after *Absence and Song*. It carries a parenthetical description after the title: "Outline of a Poem" ("Esbozo de un poema"). (III.111)[1] This description probably refers less to the physical structure of the poem than to the author's feeling that his poetic vision was incomplete. The reader inevitably associates the poem with biblical prophecy, and the account builds to the expectation of another opportunity for man; but in spite of this optimism, the poem ends on a note of doubt.

The external structure is in four cantos. The first, "The Messenger" ("El mensajero"), describes the qualities of the prophet (the Messenger) in twenty-three tercets. The second canto, "The Denunciation" ("La conminación"), consists of 116 lines of varying length and irregular stanza arrangement. The general effect is to produce a rather epic tone as compared with the lyric quality of the first canto. The third, "The Red Rain" ("La lluvia roja"), is in five-line stanzas (*quintillas*). The account of the cataclysm is given, with much movement, in these twenty stanzas. The fourth canto, "The Innocent Tribe" ("La tribu inocente"), lacks the unity of the first three. It moves from the lyric effect of tercets to the epic quality of longer and irregular lines, and is broken into several divisions, or episodes. Considering the total effect of the poem, it is fair to say that while association with ancient prophetic literature is inevitable, *The Flood of Fire* is EGM's poem and it belongs to modern times. It is the word of a poet who seeks purity in an obviously impure world.

The Messenger is to come out of solitude, out of pure essence. His origin will have nothing to do with the myth of human beginning. Having established this quality in the first tercet, the poet then writes a description of the sensitivity and natural purity of the Messenger, and reinforces the basic characteristic in the fifteenth tercet, establishing his complete purity by saying that he will not engender men. The Messenger is, therefore, entirely removed from relationship to human generations. He is a special being totally separated from the "son of death and sin" (*hijo de la muerte y el pecado*). (III.117)

Much of the description of the Messenger's sensitivity recalls EGM's poetic quest; that is, he will maintain the communication with all the things of the world—the kind of communication that is suggested by the ability to hear the silence and see the shadow. It is not surprising that the poet associates the quest with the Messenger, since the quest itself is endless, in human terms. EGM makes us feel that the quest can be brought to fruition in this special being who transcends human limitations. The Messenger will be sensitive and courageous, intuitive and rational. Before prophesying, "He will hear his own voice on the mountain" (*Oirá su propia voz en la montaña*). (III.115) Here again we see the association of the Messenger with the poetic search of EGM, because we know the significance of the authentic voice to the poet, and we have also experienced many moments of ascent through the imagery of the mountain. The feeling is the possibility of achieving what we have sought through the poetic act: an awareness of self in relation to everything else, an ability to participate with everything in the joint act of giving and receiving, and to retain this awareness of the whole, rather than feel it in a sporadic fashion. Such an accomplishment is impossible without complete purity. The Messenger's openness depends on a primordial innocence. Uncontaminated, he will be sensitive to everything, will be naked in body and spirit, so his most essential self will confront the world into which he comes.

The characteristics of the Messenger are more a catalogue than a development, since each one may be taken separately within its tercet. Each stanza emphasizes what the Messenger is like, rather than build the awareness of his nature by leading from one stanza to another. In the twenty-second tercet, the poet changes from description of the Messenger to a statement of how his coming will be known. He describes these conditions in words that suggest calm, silence, and wondering. This advent, with no blaring of trumpets, is one that we expect only a few to recognize. Certainly we would hardly expect the confused, human mass to be aware of it any more than the unseeing would be aware of the poetic search. In the next to the last tercet, EGM suggests that the Messenger will be recognized only by those with some special capacity:

> . . . A legend
> ciphered in light will name him on high
> —legible for the eye that understands—
>
> (. . . *Una leyenda*
> *cifrada en luz, lo nombrará en la altura*
> *—legible para el ojo que comprenda—.*) (III.118)

Unhappily, this wonderful impression is marred somewhat by a physical reference in the last stanza that recalls a lithograph of the stereotyped prophet with flowing hair.

The formal perfection of the tercets of the first canto contributes substantially to the feeling of perfection with regard to the Messenger, and this sense of perfection is exactly the effect that the first canto should create. Only this state of absolute purity would be appropriate for the one who so bitterly chastises men in the second canto. The difference in tone is established in the first line when the poet says that the voice will be a "roar" (*bramido*), (III.119) and the freer poetic form contributes to the strength of the utterance. The voice referred to is the Messenger's, though he is not referred to directly in the second canto. Our position is that of man who is hearing a severe dressing down, aware that the chastisement comes from an impeccable source, but concerned only subconsciously with the identification of the voice.

The voice will be both "wound and cautery" (*herida y cauterio*), (III.119) in the conscience of men. "Cautery" could be understood here either as comfort for the wound inflicted by the voice, or as punishment for evil already done. The first understanding, that the voice will have a dual effect, is eventually reinforced in the last stanza of the canto when the voice says, "At the same time I announce to you mercy and punishment" (*A la par os anuncio la piedad y el castigo*). (III.123) After the second stanza of "The Denunciation," the poem becomes a quotation of the voice which excoriates men for having vilified life. This nearly contemptuous reminder to man of his own baseness achieves a particularly meaningful statement about halfway through the canto:

> You betrayed life
> thinking that it was good only for being sung.
>
> (*Traicionasteis la vida*
> *creyendo que era buena sólo para cantarla.*) (III.121)

These lines stimulate a series of reverberating impressions in the reader who has followed the poetic journey of EGM. We think of his insistence on the meaningful rather than the purely decorative word; we remember his earnest struggle for deep communication and his impatience with his own inability to say what he discovered; we recall his inclination to separate himself from the muddled throng. But as the poem progresses, the significance of the two lines becomes more clearly defined. They are followed by a series of stanzas each beginning with a reference to some misuse of life, and ending with a reference to some kind of artistic expression that takes on the quality of sheer hypocrisy when it is seen as related to the first part of the stanza. For example, one stanza creates the feeling of the horrors of war, and ends

And you made the triumphal
poem of heroism and fatherland!

(*¡E hicisteis el poema
triunfal del heroísmo y de la patria!*) (III.121)

In this way, each of the stanzas accuses man of covering up his failure to face truth. To sing life in this fashion is indeed to betray it. The accusation does exactly what a good verbal working over should do: we begin to take account of ourselves. The denunciation is most typical of EGM when the voice says, "you never knew the profound song/ and the ineffable gift of having wings" (*ignorasteis la canción profunda/ y el inefable don de tener alas*). (III.122)

The voice becomes silent with the prediction that its words will jab the sleeping consciences, but only death will awaken them. And death comes in the cataclysm of the third canto, "The Red Rain." This is the punishment from which none escape, a punishment of flood, and fire, and blood. The intense activity of this part of the poem begins in the first stanza, even in the first word.

A sudden flame
will burst from abyss and from heights;
the imprisoned sea
will break its bonds
and bathe the plain with blood.

(*Súbita llamarada
brotará del abismo y de la altura;
la mar encadenada
romperá su clausura
y bañará de sangre la llanura.*) (III.124)

The *quintillas* communicate the violent movement well, and at the same time, their formal restriction saves the canto from melodrama, an effect which it comes very close to creating.

Many of the images used to create the sense of cataclysm suggest the implements of modern warfare:

strangely shaped winged monsters
will come down from the sky
discharging their wrath
on river, plain, and mountain.

> *(alados monstruos de figura extraña*
> *descenderán del cielo*
> *descargando su saña*
> *en el río y el llano y la montaña.)* (III.124)

Craters will be opened by "arrows of light" (*saetas de lumbre*), (III.215) and "machines with mysterious silhouettes" (*máquinas de siluetas misteriosas*), (III.125) will cross the meadow. These images are counterproductive to the effect that the third canto should produce, because we cannot accept them as prophecy. Each one suggests a tool of destruction that was perfectly well known in 1938. Rather than call them by their names, EGM alludes to them as if he were predicting their advent. He was probably trying to capture the feeling of the Apocalypse. But the imagery would be valid only if the whole poem were projected backward into the past, and then the creative effort would be of no consequence.

There are, however, images of force and destruction that are of natural origin, and these are more convincing. "The chained sea will break its boundaries" is an example of this natural force. A suggested combination of natural and man-made forces occurs in the transformation of the sea water to blood, and in other images that communicate, through reference to blood, the tragedy of wasted life. The feeling reaches a climax six stanzas from the end:

> The horizons will everywhere vomit
> serpents of blood and fire,
> and in prayerful contortion,
> masses of Laocoöns
> will people the plains and the hills.

> *(Sierpes de sangre y fuego*
> *vomitarán doquier los horizontes,*
> *y en contorsión de ruego,*
> *masas de Laocoontes*
> *poblarán las llanuras y los montes.)* (III.126-127)

The feeling at this point in the poem is one of horror, fear, and remorse. The violence is followed by the awesome silence of the wasteland which the poet expresses in the last stanza of the canto. His language of desolation is as strong as his description of violence.

The fourth canto, "The Innocent Tribe," is really in four parts. The first part, in lyrical tercets, tells of the repopulating of the earth. It has a strong flavor of patriarchal literature, and emphasizes the natural role of man—an expression of authenticity. This sense of authentic man, which permeates the first part of the canto, is well illustrated in one of the tercets which describes the wife of the tribe's leader:

> She gave him love and companionship together:
> by his priestly and fertile kiss
> became pregnant in the sunlight and gave birth joyfully.

> *(Dióle a la vez amor y compañía:*
> *de su beso hierático y fecundo*
> *preñose al sol, parió con alegría.)* (III.129)

Human authenticity, as it develops here, involves the rediscovery of values that are more or less primitive. And the word "primitive" has to be modified, because the common understanding of it tends to vary with the purpose for which it is used: it could refer to cavemen, or to a nomadic society, or even to a sedentary society that is still relatively simple. A circumstance of simple uncomplicated living is the essential communication of EGM's poem. The feeling is that man in this state is still aware of his proximity to nature. He still knows, for example, the relationship of food to his own effort and the maintenance of life. His basic need (food) is not separated from its effect (sustenance) by a series of intermediate steps imposed by the complications of society. Therefore, he sees more clearly what he is. And although man in this state is already removed from the condition of purity that is the ideal in many of EGM's poems, he is still sufficiently aware of his nature to be very different from the muddled throng of advanced civilization.

The theme of "the nature of things" is carried on in the second part of the canto, but in a different setting. The prophetic voice speaks again, and the poetic line changes to make its admonition more impressive. The voice rededicates the world to the use of men, to the new men who may see what the others never saw. The idea of authenticity is developed in a series of stanzas that relate the acts of unsophisticated men to the social benefits of a more complicated society. EGM uses, for example, the image of sowing the seed, and it becomes the seed of truth that will produce peace and justice which are the food and drink of living together. These stanzas cause us to feel that man must not lose his sensitivity to his basic reality, and they lead directly into an exhortation to creativity.

> Create, create miracles of color and of line,
> of song and of word . . .
>
> *(Cread, cread milagros de color y de línea,*
> *de cántico y de verbo.)* (III.132)

The third part of the canto becomes a concentration on creativity. The exhortation is to acute awareness of everything, and is very similar in feeling to many of the earlier poems of González Martínez. Unlike those poems in which the address is to the singular "you," the advice here is given in the plural, and the feeling is less intimate. But there is no doubt that the poet hopes that men will comprehend life more fully.

> Run always ahead, fishers of dreams,
> shepherds of deep solitudes,
> secret hunters of silences . . .
>
> *Corred siempre adelante, pescadores de sueños,*
> *pastores de las hondas soledades,*
> *cazadores furtivos de silencios . . .)* (III.134)

The Messenger retires to the mountain, and all that remains of the poem is the fourth part of the last canto, which consists of only eight lines. They amount to a sort of promise or covenant. The Messenger will be found on the heights, but the poet's description of him casts doubt on the probability of man's following the admonitions.

It would be less than honest to end the discussion of *The Flood of Fire* without calling attention to an idea which is clearly contrary to this reading of the poem, but which may have some validity. In the fourth stanza of the second part of the last canto, the prophetic voice speaks to the new men concerning their place of origin. In ten lines he describes a geographical utopia, with a strong sense of the everlasting quality of nature and an equally strong suggestion of creation. The description of rivers, mountains, lakes, flowers, and the like is stated in language that might conceivably be understood to refer to Latin America. In other words, it is possible to react to this passage in such a way that the poem becomes a promise of the emergence of the new people in Latin America. Such is probably not what EGM intended to say, for two reasons: first, human origin is commonly associated with a beneficent land, and EGM's description is not precise enough to be conclusive evidence; second, the poet's concern throughout his work is universal rather than regional. However, we cannot overlook the fact that many Latin-American writers, since the turn of the century, have thought and written a great deal about the destiny of Latin America; and one of the best-known essays is José Vasconcelos' "The Cosmic Race" ("La raza cós-mica"), 1925, which hypothesizes that Latin America will be the birthplace of the "fifth race," the "non-race."[2] Although the problem of race does not enter specifically into "The Denunci-ation," EGM does specify it in *Babel*.

II Babel

Babel was published in 1949, one year after *Thistle in the Wind*.[3] It was the last volume of EGM's poetry published before the year of his death, when *The New Narcissus* appeared. It is important to note that the poet's concern for mankind, after the experience of the Second World War, prompted him to act as chairman of the organizational committee of the American Continental Peace Conference. In *Second Awakening*, which was published in 1945, EGM included an honestly vengeful poem, "Prayer in Time of War" ("Oración en la guerra"), in which there is no attempt to soften the poet's desire for retribu-tion. His prayer, stated simply and unpoetically, is that he may live long enough to see suitable punishment meted out to the ignominious "buffoon" (*histrión*), (*Sec. Awak.* XXVI), who started the holocaust. He wants to see "mire return to mire and death to death" (*el fango vuelva al fango y la muerte a la muerte*). (*Sec. Awak.* XXVI) It is significant that he uses the word "death" in this case—it communicates the darkness and despair that the poet saw in this misuse of men, and of life. The first three of five quatrains are devoted to the vengeance desired; the last two, to the restoration of harmony among men, and the reign of peace. It is then that the poet will be ready to give up his concern for men. We also find a specifically stated change in the author's position when, looking forward to the return of harmony, he anticipates also "an *our* life that once was only *mine*" (*una vida* nuestra *que antes fué sólo* mía). (*Sec. Awak.* XXVI) This line is EGM's most specific poetic statement of commitment to the world of social confusion.

There are enough political allusions in *Babel* to relate it clearly to the poet's concern for the world; but his hope is for change that is far more profound—and in that sense, far more radical—than the political proclamation of international accord. *Babel* is subtitled "Poem on the margin of time" ("Poema al margen del tiempo") because it is written in the poet's state of suspension between heights and abyss. Here the facets of chronology are united and the poem becomes a universal vision. Even the specific references to temporal facts are intended to extend into timelessness.

The external structure of *Babel* is extremely simple. It is a series of fourteen poems, thematically related, and written predominantly in linked tercets. EGM varies the form in only three of the fourteen poems—in each case to gain dramatic emphasis through a less lyric verse. Each poem is numbered and titled. The first is "Prelude of Evasion" ("Preludio de evasión"), which frees us from the restrictions of visible reality without detaching us from it, and sets the stage for a visionary experience.

The poem is written in the past tense, and the reader's first assumption is that, after a prologue, the author will change to present tense. When it becomes apparent that the past tense is maintained generally throughout the poem, since it is really a recounting of a vision experienced, the prelude itself becomes part of the vision. In the first line, the poet views "the hard earth" (*la dura tierra*), (57) which evokes in us a sense of its durability and tangibleness. Here the poet has experienced both anguish and hope, and feels strongly attached to this material aspect of reality. In expressing this attachment, he establishes the basic image of this first poem: the earth is the plant, the poet its flower. In the next four lines, the roots extend downward, the flower reaches up. So living in both directions at once, the poet communicates his dual commitment. While the plant enjoys the nourishment of earth, its flower (the poet) reaches toward the heavens "like a winged heart that bleeds" (*como un alado corazón que sangra*). (57) The bleeding heart communicates the intense desire of the search; it means the actual expenditure of life.

Up to this point in the poem, the reader is likely to identify with EGM in the sense that he knows what the poet is feeling; then, in the next line, the reader begins to participate in the feeling, when the physical image becomes emotion. Now, the flower becomes "the floral craving" (*la floral avidez*), (57) and the emotion becomes more important than the physical components of the image. The reader becomes a part of the craving which reaches up "in search of invisible universes, new suns and new souls" (*en busca de invisibles universos, de nuevos soles y de nuevas almas*). (57) This seeker of new worlds, now a combination of poet, reader, image (flower), and emotion (craving), comes from "a sad world in which love is disappearing" (*un mundo triste en que el amor acaba*), (57) and expects to be refreshed in a new world where there are "undreamed-of forests" (*selvas no soñadas*), (57) and where waits "the bird that came out of the ark" (*el ave que salió del arca*). (58) The two expectations suggest a world completely different from the one circumscribed by visible reality, one that can be achieved only in a state of purity. The bird, a symbol of purity, awaits the cleansing of the bloody plain—a figure that evokes the anguish of man's misuse of life, so vividly created in *The Flood of Fire*. EGM's prelude moves toward an anticipation of purity.

The second poem, "Apparition" ("Aparición"), is written in carefully disciplined, linked tercets (the blank line of one tercet becomes the rhyming line of the next), and introduces the source of the voice that will speak during the visionary experience. EGM describes a mystical presence, stating her advent (the presence is feminine) in the past tense, then shifting to the present in order to incorporate the reader into his awareness of the force exerted on him by the presence. The union of the two is felt throughout the poem, particularly in "Her eyes in mine" (*Sus ojos en los míos*), (58) and later in "I feel her fine hand on my heart" (*siento pegada al corazón su fina mano*). (59)

The origin of the presence is as uncontaminated as the origin of the Messenger.

> In her incorporeal majesty, she came
> from a world of phantoms, or death
> returned her to give me company.

> (*En su incorpórea majestad, venía
> de un mundo de fantasmas o la muerte
> la devolvió por darme compañía.*) (58)

This description of her coming follows a stanza where the poet compares her advent with the coming of dawn. Now, in the present verse, he suggests the return of the lost beloved. However, such a definitive identification would lead to an inadequate reading of the poem. The presence may also be regarded as muse, inspiration, or spirit; and just as we recognize a lack of definition among these three, so we may also include the beloved whom we have seen in other poems as a road to poetic discovery, especially in "Ballad of the Living Dead." The poem ends with a reiterated awareness of the presence accompanied by the fear that she might leave. Her departure would, of course, leave the vision incomplete. The last line suggests that she might be "dissolved in the flight of hours" (*disuelta en la fuga de las horas*), (59) an image which reinforces the basic characteristic of *Babel*: its existence on the margin of time. The flight of segmented time would destroy the vision.

The poet's reaction to the mysterious presence is enlarged in "Revelation" ("Revelación"), which continues the tercets of the preceding poem. The tone is much the same, with the stress on the function rather than on the origin of the presence. She speaks for the first time in this poem and identifies herself in two stages of clarification: in the first stage, the feeling is more maternal; in the second stage, it is wifely. The most important aspect of the poem is the feeling of constancy that it develops. At the end, the revelation of her identity is completed by the quotation of three lines from "Life in Defeat," one of the poems from *Thistle in the Wind*. Here she is a "providential traveller" (*providencial viajera*), (61) who comes to help the poet with smile and tears at the end of his career. This quotation identifies the presence as the one of the earlier poems mentioned, and of several others. This revelation, of course, is not very helpful to the reader who would have her say "I am your wife," or "I am your soul," or "I am your muse." However, "Revelation" is a beautiful development of the poet's feeling of constant assurance that the poetic road is open.

The poet ascends with her in "Ascension" ("Ascensión") and reaches the sapphire mountain. The quality of the adjective here confers brilliant firmness to the poetic quest and changes it from the rather vague state of the first poem where the reaching out is contrasted with the hardness of earth. Here he is sustained by his inspiration and finds himself in a position to view the world.

> An invisible hand showed me heaven's
> divine breath that comforts
> the mortal tribe that walks the earth.
>
> (*Mano invisible me mostró del cielo*
> *el hálito divino que conforta*
> *a la tribu mortal que pisa el suelo.*) (62)

At this point the poet looks at the earth and says that "its agony came to me more deeply" (*me llegó más honda su agonía*). (62) He expresses this agony in the image of a serpent embracing and crushing earth. This serpent is the power of evil, and the first section of "Ascension" ends with a statement of the poet's reaction to the world's misery: "And I saw its anguish and felt it the more mine" (*Y ví su angustia y la sentí más mía*). (62)

In the second section, the chaotic, contaminated state of the world breaks the walls of EGM's solitude. The poet, standing exposed to the effects of evil and in full communion now with the agonizing world, turns to questions: "What dark shadow blinded the shepherd and scattered the flock?" (*¿Qué sombra densa cegó al pastor y dispersó al rebaño?*), (63) a query that communicates the inevitable feeling of disintegration among those who cannot see their fundamental unity. The response is partially contained in another question that asks why there is not love instead of a river of weeping. It is apparent that disintegration is a loveless state; and, of course, this question recalls the image of the flower that escapes from a world where love is disappearing, in "Prelude of Evasion." Is there no power that will overcome evil? Has the poet lost faith in the efficacy of his word? And where is the prophet?

In the third part of "Ascension," EGM creates the contrast between purity and corruption. The sea is the source of life and the symbol of primordial innocence. That sea now "rises in waves of blood" (*en olas de sangre se levanta*). (64) Just as in the "Prelude of Evasion," the blood here is a reminder of man's misuse of life.

The title of the fifth poem, "Vision" ("Visión"), suggests that it probably contains the nucleus of *Babel*. Certainly the whole work is visionary. The poems of the appearance and revelation of the presence are a part of the total experience; and the ascent with her reveals to the poet the anguish of the world caught in the grip of evil. In "Vision," the nature of evil is more specifically defined. The poet views "the macabre parade of death" (*el macabro desfile de la muerte*). (64)

In the second stanza, death becomes war in the suggestion of red and of ruins and spoils. The feeling is of death passing over a devastated earth. The reference to death as "mute phantom" (*mudo fantasma*), (64) begins a development of the inexorable

course of death, carried on in the third stanza through the concept of death crossing a plain that is desolate and endless. Then
in the fourth tercet, death continues on its course, taking no
heed of the accusation of fratricide. We feel, therefore, a combination of fear and revulsion before a completely inhuman
force, an abstract destructive power that goes on and on. However, in the last two stanzas of "Vision," EGM turns our reaction
toward a more tangible object when he sees Cain—human, guilty,
malevolent, tortured. But we do not come to feel that the act
of Cain is one that can be regarded in isolation, or as having
found its expiation. Rather, the human particularity of Cain
combines with the abstraction of death in the earlier verses, and
the result is an exceptionally full appreciation of the myth. We
feel that Cain goes on reproducing himself endlessly, that there
is something in man that is at once hateful and inevitable.

The following poem, "Interrogation" ("Interrogación"), changes the poetic form for the first time since "Prelude of Evasion"
and uses a longer line in assonance when an unidentified voice
speaks in a way quite similar to "The Denunciation" of *The
Flood of Fire.* The questions turn into accusation and build on
the feeling of hopeless revulsion that is the emotional climax of
"Vision." The question is what force causes men to seek their
own destruction. Because the questions come out of the agony
of the preceding poem, where the reader has become intimately
involved, they seem to be the reader's own questions. At the
end of the first stanza, when the questions change to accusation,
EGM sees the fratricidal—and by extension, suicidal—tendency
of men as a perversion of natural harmony.

> Your life is a song of violated notes
> that a madman rehearses without harmony or rhythm.
>
> (*Vuestra vida es un canto de atropelladas notas
> que un lunático ensaya sin acorde y sin ritmo.*) (65)

This is an important image because it means that the poet's
anguish is based not on a limited view of the social organism,
but on the function of man in relation to the universe.

In the succeeding lines of the accusation, the voice speaks
of the influence of false gods—an influence that has had the
effect of dividing men, by races and by geography. The poet
strengthens the feeling of tragedy by contrasting man's divisiveness with nature's unity, bringing the noise of strife into conflict
with natural harmony.

> You stopped the course of the golden days
> when all was ours and not yours or mine
>
> *(Detuvisteis el paso de las horas doradas
> en que todo era nuestro y no tuyo ni mío.)*

In the last line of "Interrogations," the blood which is mentioned in preceding poems of *Babel* is identified as the "blood of false heroism" (*sangre de mendaz heroismo*). (66)

In the seventh poem, "Dialogue on the Heights" ("Diálogo en la altura"), the poet returns to linked tercets and communicates the conflict between his desire to continue the ascent, and the obligation to return to the human muddle. Actually, the poem is not much of a dialogue: it is written in six parts, with the poet asking the question in the first part, and the presence making her response in the following five parts. "Dialogue on the Heights" is the weakest poem in *Babel,* because it undertakes a justification of the author's social commitment, and throughout most of the poem, we watch EGM struggle with what he wants to say, rather than participate in the development of the poetic emotion. The fourth part is an exception, because within it we feel the growth of the importance of the poetic act.

In the first part, the basic question is posed. The words chosen by the poet to present the contrast between the extremes of his choice indicate clearly what his preference would be. It is a choice between silence and noise, between purity and contamination. His reference to the "red mire of the impure earth" (*fango rojo de la tierra impura*), (67) carries the unwelcome message of hate and of blindness that is the general view of earth in *Babel.* Then in the last stanza, the poet feels the reassurance of the presence and is prepared to hear her voice.

When the presence speaks, in the second part, she tells the poet immediately that he must return to the anguish of earth rather than seek distant peace and love. Within the admonition itself, the voice refers to earthly corruption in images that stress again the unnatural quality of man's evil. But in the last stanza, she assures the poet that love grows even in the midst of contamination. The third part continues the assurance of love's persistence, in the imagery of bud and grain, and moves to her statement of the poet's impregnability. He can expect to be attacked by evil, but the very fact that he is a poet will protect him from evil's effect.

The voice appears to digress at the beginning of the fourth part, asking why humans have set up divisions that divide some men from others. The basis of the question here is why use the terms "east and west" (*oriente y occidente*). (69) The question carries the implication of natural human unity, and develops into further assurance to the poet that he can promote this unity. From the assumption of natural unity, the emotion develops toward the need for someone to remind men of it, then to the feeling that the poetic word is not lost, and finally to an awareness of the pervasive quality of what the poet says.

The fifth part continues the theme of human disunity, stressing here the division by race rather than by geographical boundaries. Man the exploiter, the spoiler, goes on engendering himself forever, maintaining his unnatural divisiveness, racial, political, religious. In the sixth part, the presence tells the poet again that he must descend to the confusion of the world, but she also speaks of his special condition: he is to build his own tower in the blackness. He maintains his poetic integrity by seeing more deeply than those about him, by being extremely sensitive to the whole reality.

"Confusion" ("Confusión") is the beginning of the poet's descent into the world of men. The feeling in the first two stanzas communicates confidence and a certain desire to make amends for his "timid flight" (*fuga cerval*). (71) The third stanza also communicates the poet's regret that his sorrow caused him to separate himself from the world. Now recommitted, EGM expresses the desire to attend the needs of men, to calm their anguish, to dress their wounds. Most of all he wants to place signposts that will give men direction. Here, even without the poet's statement, we feel again the sense of natural harmony, the state in which men would know their direction.

Although the poet assumes the task of pointing the way, EGM asks, in three stanzas beginning with the eighth: What worldly sign will mark the road? In these lines, all interrogative, the poet lists descriptively a number of symbols of political power: the hammer and sickle, the half moon, the bald eagle, the eagle and serpent, and others. Certainly these lines must be remembered when we mention the social and political meaning of *Babel*. But we should understand very clearly that their use is more social than political. There is no reason at all to believe that EGM is seeking, among these symbols, the one that will

lead men upward. Rather, the implication is that none of them
will, because what they really symbolize is divisiveness, greed,
and hate. This feeling is evoked in the present poem by the
statement, in the ninth stanza, that hate stanches the spring.
But the final stanza contains the balancing optimism: love
flourishes in the sun that lights the day and kisses the seed. The
emotion at the end of the poem is that love, however hidden
in the world, is always on the verge of bursting forth.

"Disillusion" ("Desilusión") is the action of the poet among
men. The author states the reason for disillusionment in the
first line and in very direct fashion: "I spoke; but my language
was lost" (*Hablé; pero mi lengua se perdía*). (73) The noise
of other tongues drowns out the poetic voice that would indicate
the direction. One of the destructive words is "race" (*raza*),
another is "fatherland" (*patria*); (73) one leads to slavery, the
other to the concept of enemy. Both divide men. EGM moves
from this general view to the recall of specific acts that communicate man's lack of reason. One states the people's choice
of Barrabas over Jesus, another cites the death of Gandhi. These
incidents are a part of the visionary experience, and it is well
to remember that *Babel* is a poem written "on the margin of
time."

The people repudiate truth. Moving from these specific acts,
the poet returns to generalization and sees that all power becomes tyranny. Certainly we feel here that the references to
worldly power, in the preceding poem, suggest no choice, nor
even hope. At this point we feel something approaching self-
betrayal, as if some human deficiency is driving us to our own
destruction. There is a tragic misdirection—we know that everything is going awry; and we join the poet in saying, "And my
hope trembled on the way" (*Y tembló mi esperanza en el
camino*). (74)

"Promise" ("Promisión") refers specifically to the conflicting
forces of the Second World War; but again we must be careful
not to allow ourselves to be limited by the historical reference,
because the poet carefully makes the incident transcendent, and
maintains the poem on the margin of time. EGM goes back to
the longer line in "Promise," in search of a more heroic tone,
but he does use consonantal rhyme. St. John appears before the
poet in the first lines and bids him to "come and see" (*ven y
mira*). (75) EGM refers to him as "the seer of Patmos" (*el

vidente de Patmos), (75) and thereby suggests a similarity to the Book of Revelation which, according to tradition, St. John wrote on the island of Patmos. The rolling lines of "Promise" do indeed capture something of the feeling of the Apocalypse, and the general sense of the poem is appropriate to that kind of literature. In general, apocalyptic literature reassures a troubled people that their enemies will be punished and their own future will be brighter.

The major part of "Promise" is a comparison of two horsemen. One is warlike and inspired by Satan. He carries a banner on which appears the Christian symbol with its points bent, a reference to the swastika (an earlier reference to this horseman as "blond" now becomes a symbol of Nazism). However, the last lines of the description are more meaningful than the identification of the rider with Nazi terror, because they inform us that the Angel of Death rides with him. Our reaction to the poem expands immediately, because now we associate the rider with more than a single incident in history.

The other horseman is categorically differentiated from his opponent, even by the color and demeanor of his mount—the horse is white and moves with deliberation. The second rider wears the laurel and his standard bears the "V" for victory. The use in the poem of this symbol of the Allies during the Second World War is likely to evoke a somewhat adverse reaction from the reader—at least from the reader who lived through it and experienced the use of the symbol as commonplace, daily propaganda. But the horseman speaks to the poet and informs him that, for those who look deeply, the "V" is also for "Truth" (*Verdad*). (76) The poet has again transcended the limitations of a specific incident. Entering the poem to the fullest extent, we now have the feeling of struggle between death and truth.

It is amply evident that the anticipated victory is considerably more significant than the downfall of Nazi madness. The fact is only a symbol of the more fundamental problem. At the end of the second horseman's words, he promises victory over the other. The last three lines of the poem communicate an air of expectancy, appreciated by the poet, but ignored by the masses of men. They depart into the shadow, which is the opposite of the promised victory of truth.

Face to face with the insensitivity of men, in "Vacillation" ("Vacilación"), the poet wonders what he is supposed to do.

Returning to linked tercets, EGM develops the condition of blind confusion in the first five stanzas. As he often does in building an emotion, he moves from general to particular and back to general. Men who neither see nor hear are particularized in specific examples—for instance, of the mother who leads her progeny by one hand and lifts the other against both her brother and her father. Then back to the generality. All men move endlessly and blindly, muttering "in an absurd, sonorous confusion" (*en una absurda confusión sonora*). (77) The poet then takes account, in specific reference, of the man who spoke of love, but whose voice was lost in the worldly noise. Returning to the generality of anguish, the poet asks the mystical presence what he should do. The promise of the preceding poem appears to have come to nothing. He wonders if he should go away and wait for a time when either he can understand the language of men or they can understand him. The question is followed by a single line that ends the poem: "And I read the answer in her glance" (*Y leí la respuesta en su mirada*). (78) Although we may guess what the answer is, the device amounts to the use of suspense to carry the reader forward into the next poem. Unhappily, it tends to alienate the reader who, by this time, is likely to be completely caught up in the flow of the poet's emotion.

Clarification comes in several different ways in "Redemption" ("Redención"). The poem is divided into three parts, and in the first the mystical presence addresses the poet concerning his own purity. With a firm gentleness, the voice reminds the poet that he must free himself from his own tyrannies. The revelation of the poet's state reaches its climax in

> How wrest hate from the earth,
> how climb with cherub wings,
> if war is deep within your heart?
>
> (*¿Cómo arrancar el odio de la tierra,*
> *cómo ascender con alas de querube*
> *si está en mitad del corazón la guerra?*) (79)

The problem is not just how to bring truth to men, but how to remove hate from the earth so truth may reign. Even the warrior of truth in "Promise" revealed a vindictive attitude; and EGM's earlier poem, "Prayer in Time of War," speaks in no uncertain terms of the poet's desire for retribution against the man who caused such suffering.

The second part of "Redemption" contains the direct answer
to the question raised in "Vacillation." The flight proposed by
the poet is a foolish idea because it presupposes a sequence of
segments of time that would make it possible for him to do one
thing now and another thing later. Actually, there is no "now"
and "later."

> "Flee in order to return?   Vain word!
> Today is an artifice of the mind,
> yesterday is nonsense, tomorrow is shadow.
>   "Only eternity is present,
> and universal anxiety and your destiny
> go eternally in pursuit of love . . ."
>
>   ("*¿Huír para volver?   ¡Palabra vana!*
> *El hoy es artificio de la mente,*
> *devaneo el ayer, sombra el mañana.*
>   "*Sólo la eternidad está presente,*
> *y el ansia universal y tu destino*
> *van en pos del amor eternamente . . .*") (79)

She informs the poet that the divine is reached by means of
the human, and advises him "to live immensity in the depth of
mortal life" (*vive la immensidad en lo profundo de la vida
mortal*). (80)

A substantial part of the last section of "Redemption" should
be wordless, but the poet has no alternative to words. His purpose is to reproduce his wondering about what force causes
the misuse of life. He says that his question was formed without
words. The best the reader can do is absorb the spirit of the
poet's questioning into his own emotion. The poet's questions
are addressed to the point of experience where human shadow
and divine light are joined (the point of understanding that
synthesizes the poles of his poetic quest). He comprehends that
the reason why men lose direction is contained within life itself.
He then feels the agony of men through intimate communion,
just as many years before he found communion with the things
of the universe in "You Will Pass Over the Life of Things," and
his reaction is different from the bitterness felt when he views
man from the heights. By means of this deep communion, he
now knows that he can ascend—not in spite of human agony,
but because of it.

"Daydream" ("Ensoñación") is the most beautiful poem of
Babel because it expresses, in parallel imagery, the reunion of

all creation. Within the recounting of the vision, the poet dreams, and he sees man in brotherly communion, belonging to one fatherland, joining in one prayer. Within each, love has lighted the same fire; but this fire is more universal than one shared by men. It is the fire that lights the stars, that warms the hearth, that cheers the wayfarer, that brightens a face. It is a "Pentecost of collective flame" (*pentecostés de colectiva llama*), (82) and it is its own vestal, its own guardian. EGM's use of these images develops the poem to the point of an overwhelming sense of perpetual harmony.

The vision comes to an end in "Suspension" ("Suspensión"). The mystical presence has vanished. The poet thinks she may be calling him from the heights, but he no longer has the certainty of feeling her presence. He is still the man he was, and he does not know whether to return to strifetorn, worldly life, or follow the impulse of his own yearning. But then the indecision becomes pointless, because his wings lack the vigor for the ascent, and his feet are fearful of descending. He is here, as in many poems, suspended between the two poles:

> Like a floating cloud of incense
> that does not reach the empty dome,
> between earth and azure suspended,
> I am still the plaything of the air.

> (*Como flotante nébula de incienso*
> *que no alcanza la cúpula vacía,*
> *entre la tierra y el azul, suspenso,*
> *soy juguete del aire todavía.*) (83)

III Beginning and End of the Sea

Dated 1950, *Beginning and End of the Sea* (*Principio y fin del mar*) appears in the volume entitled *The New Narcissus*, where it is part of a trilogy that also contains *Babel* and *The Flood of Fire*. Although it is considerably shorter than the two earlier poems (it has twenty-six quatrains), it clearly deserves to be considered as an independent work, but related to the other poems of social commitment. It is divided into two parts, a first part of eight stanzas and a second part of eighteen. The verse form is consistent throughout, as is the lyric quality. The thematic development of the poem does not require variety of form. It is divided into two parts in order to emphasize a

contrast that is the basis of the poem. Indeed, it is subtitled
"Poem in Two Dreams" ("Poema en dos sueños").

The first part of the poem creates a mood of silence, serenity,
purity, absolute perfection. The sea is primordial, original, preceded only by its own creation, if such can be called an act
of precedence. The only suggestion that there was anything
before the sea is the statement that it was "wept by the eye of
an unfathomable eternity" (*por el ojo de una insondable
eternidad llorada*). (84) The poet begins by saying, "I dreamed
of a sea recently born" (*Yo soñé con un mar recién nacido*), (84)
then intensifies the feeling of origin through a progression of
images. It is in "uncorrupted solitude" (*impoluta soledad*), (84)
and it is quiet and innocent. Its innocence is reinforced after
an interval of two stanzas by

> maidenhood of crystal that is horrified
> by the possible violation of a voyage.

> *(doncellez de cristal que se horroriza*
> *de la posible violación de un viaje.)* (85)

We feel both the primordial and cosmic implications of "Water
asleep in celestial prelude" (*Aqua en preludio sideral dormida*).
(84) Above all, it is the absence of the human touch that ac-
counts for the sea's perfection. It is self-contained, unadulterated
existence. The feeling is similar to that of the poems in which
EGM creates a state of pure being—open, vulnerable, yet imperturbable. The poet brings the virginal unity of the sea to
concluding intensity in the last stanza of the first part, by using
images that recapitulate the emotions of the preceding stanzas.
Its silence and its undisturbed surface are summed up in "dia-
mond quietude" (*diamantina quietud*). (85) The smooth surface
carries over into an expression of the sea's integrity—its unity,
that is—in "mirror of itself" (*espejo de sí propio*). (85) The
virginal state is reiterated in "paradise of the fountain" (*paraíso
de la fuente*), (85) an image which also suggests its stillness.
The paradise or sinless state of water is the state of calm before
it is disturbed by action. The poetic emotion is the same as that
of "Nascent Soul," from *Second Awakening*.

The mood of the second part is quite different, because here
the emotion moves from awareness of action, to confusion, then
to chaos, and finally to cataclysm. Although the progression
begins with the first line of the second part, "And I saw that

the water was tinted with red" (*Y ví que el agua se tiñó de rosa*), (85) the change is not abrupt but is very gradual, just as suggested by the verb "tinted." Within the same stanza we feel a threat to the water's virginity.

The next two stanzas relate the creation of the world. The poetic effect is to create the sense of movement, of activity that destroys the primordial integrity of the sea. The first sun rises, the winds begin, the earth moves beneath the waters. The poet's reference to "evil gods" (*malignos dioses*), (86) evokes a sense of foreboding with regard to the corruption of innocence. Then the activities of men join the activities of nature, and Pandora's box is opened. The face of death appears.

EGM uses both nature and mythological references to intensify the sense of the role of man and the end of purity. The feeling is that man, simply by being what he is—or at best, urged on by a force he does not understand—contaminates the world. As his activity increases, "the heavens are covered by signs and tokens/ that augur danger and forecast hate" (*cubren los cielos signos y presagios/ que auguran riesgos y predicen odio*). (87) By the middle of the second part, the imagery has changed completely from the purity of the first part, to expressions of suffering, horror, tragedy, brutality. Throughout this development, EGM is careful to use the sea as his basic image, so the reader is constantly aware of the contrast between the perfection of Part One and the growing confusion of Part Two.

In two stanzas, the poet refers to the role of the sea in biblical history: the flood and the exodus. The stanza on the flood shows the wrathful sea attempting to purify man, but the new world that comes out of the ark contains evil. The emotion in this stanza is the same as the emotion of uncertainty that is revealed in the Messenger at the end of *The Flood of Fire*. The stanza on the exodus shows the sea, clearly the symbol of natural harmony, trying to save good and destroy evil by choosing one people over another; but the people redeemed by the sea wander the earth without security.

In the last quarter of the second part, a reference to modern warfare—"armored fish" (*pez blindado*) (88)— suggests man's insistent perversity. Sinful man is more and more separated from his natural state until he loses direction entirely. In the imagery of a compass that has lost its north, we feel the quality of human confusion. Indeed, man becomes so disoriented that he commits

the ultimate anti-natural act when "he breaks and spreads abroad
the eternal secret/ that marks the rhythm in which the earth
rocks" (*rompe y divulga el eterno secreto/ que marca el ritmo
en que se mece el orbe*). (88) At first this seems to be a most
extraordinary statement in the poetry of an artist who searched
so ardently for the eternal secret. But then we recall that the
poet also feels that the secret is indeed eternal, and that while
the search is inevitable for those who would live profoundly, it
is the search rather than the discovery that is desirable. In some
poems, it is clear that his real hope is the attainment of a state
of purity. The will to live is what is really durable, and the
ideal is the purest conceivable life. The first part of *Beginning
and End of the Sea* communicates the feeling of this ideal.

Our reaction to the contrast between purity and contamination,
deepened now by a sense of betrayal, becomes an emotional
reverberation, even though we don't know exactly what the
poet means by this exposure of the eternal secret. Then we
move to the last stanza and the first line informs us: "I saw the
natural rhythm of the atom violated" (*Ví la euritmia del átomo
violada*). (88) The key word here is *euritmia*. It has an English
cognate, "eurythmy," which is hopelessly unpoetic and something
less than commonly used. The word communicates harmonious
movement, and that is why EGM uses it here, rather than simply
"rhythm" (*ritmo*). The feeling is that proportion has been destroyed. There is no suggestion of an anti-scientific position here.
Indeed, it may be well to recall that the poet was trained in the
sciences, and certainly this training must have been a part of
the reason for his not accepting a facile explanation of the
mystery of the continuity of life. What we feel here is not a
condemnation of investigation, but the horror of man's ability
to open up a secret that escapes his control. The poet feels that
man has not just discovered the universe, he had found a way
to change its nature. The result is a holocaust.

Now, at the end of the poem, the artist reasserts the sea
imagery, and when it is mentioned, we recall its perfection in
Part One. But the impression is brief, because these lines are
different:

> The sea on the moribund planet
> was an evaporated, azure tear.
>
> (*El mar sobre el planeta moribundo
> fue una lágrima azul evaporada.*) (89)

IV *The Search Suspended*

Enrique González Martínez died in 1952. His song and search had lasted more than half a century. Throughout his poetry he travelled the road toward a sense of universal integration, and the journey was characterized by his intimate communion with the things of the world. Yet in spite of this poetic consistency, it is helpful to see his work in three periods. The early period (1895-1920) was the time of discovery of himself as a poet when, after some preliminary work, he sensed the profound relationship between himself and the universe. The middle period (1921-1934) corresponds more or less to the time of his ambassadorship, when his work was affected, though not deeply influenced, by vanguardist poetry. The final period (1935-1952) is the time of the poetry of sorrow and commitment. This poetry is to a considerable extent a return to the poetry of the early period.

Given the unusual chronological span of EGM's poetry, literary historians are confronted with the problem of where to place him most meaningfully in the panorama of Mexican letters. The solution has generally been to place him among the *modernistas*, with some explanation of the decision. The poet himself was never able to understand why he was so placed, and the problem is complicated by the fact that EGM spoke out against the brilliant superficialities of *modernista* verse. There is no doubt, however, that his first poems belong there; and it is equally certain that he felt a strong attachment to the French poets who inspired *modernismo*, as evidenced by his translations and his teaching.

The crux of the matter appears to lie in the influence of Symbolism on EGM's work. Both Parnassianism and Symbolism inspired *modernista* poetry. Generally speaking, the Parnassian phase belongs to the years before 1896, the Symbolist phase to the later years of the movement. EGM obviously belongs to the Symbolist phase; but in addition to this chronological fact, Symbolism was for him a deeper experience than it was for most *modernista* poets. That is to say, the physical objects of the material world symbolized spiritual truth for him, and this correspondence was the basis of his poetry. EGM's objection to *modernismo* was directed against superficial brilliance, not against the profound search. Although the period of *modernismo* is generally considered to have ended by 1920, it should be clear that EGM never deserted Symbolism. As we move into the poetry that sometimes bears the paradoxical name *postmodernismo*, we find that the intimate search of EGM places him in a group of similar Spanish-American poets, like Rafael Alberto Arrieta of Argentina and Magallanes Moure of Chile. It would be difficult to establish the direction of influences among these poets.

González Martínez established the basic characteristics of his poetry during the early period, and his contributions to Mexican literature can be seen most clearly through comparison with some of his contemporaries. For several years prior to 1920, the two great voices in Mexican poetry were those of EGM and Ramón López Velarde (1888-1921). Even if we consider the latter to be the child of *modernismo*, he was not rooted in it as González Martínez was. Both poets were writing at a time when their country was struggling through a major social revolution. One of the products of the revolution was a conflict between cultural cosmopolitanism and cultural nationalism. López Velarde showed how a focus on his provincial background —on circumstances that are characteristically Mexican—could be enlarged to universal significance. For EGM, however, this question never arose. His poetry always transcended national boundaries, and he was keenly aware of the relationship of his work to the European tradition. His calm and absolute acceptance of this fact strengthened the position of those poets who fought to maintain the great tradition of poetry while others proposed an extreme social commitment that often produced propaganda.

We may identify "the great tradition of poetry" as the impulse to discover always a deeper truth through the poetic act. EGM's contribution in this direction may be seen clearly in a comparison with Amado Nervo (1870-1919); and such a comparison is inevitable because moral value is associated with the work of both men. Since neither of them was able to accept his orthodox, traditional faith, they were faced with the search for meaning. Throughout his lifetime, Nervo moved from one set of beliefs to another, and his poems are expositions of propositions which constitute the basis of the poetry. González Martínez, on the other hand, discovers the proposition through the poetic act. His poetry never offers the false comfort that we find in Nervo's, but it upholds the validity of the constant, if agonizing, search.

The value of this search—one might say it is the only reality—passes from one true poet to another, perhaps more subconsciously than otherwise.

The great innovator of EGM's time was Juan José Tablada (1871-1945), and with regard to new forms and new themes, he was far more influential than González Martínez. Tablada travelled extensively, read extensively, and was a kind of literary sponge. There was hardly any poetic tendency of his time that is not visible somewhere in Tablada's work. He was a facile poet rather than a great one, but his artistic extroversion enabled him to stimulate younger writers toward inventiveness. His influence and contribution are more apparent than EGM's, but they are not more important.

González Martínez was never an innovator. His favorite and most successful form was the sonnet. He did use form very effectively; but his usage is subtle, and intended for his own purposes, rather than for stimulating other poets. Even his excellent imagery is restrained, and is used for his own discovery of communion with the universe. In the middle period, when he had come to know vanguardist poetry, he did change a bit, became more objective. But even then he was involved with the things of the universe, rather astonished by them.

It is probable that the late teens and early twenties were the period of EGM's greatest direct influence on other poets. That is, those were the years when the largest number of poets read his work and listened carefully to what he was saying. When he returned to Mexico at the end of his ambassadorship, he was by age and honor the dean of Mexican poets, but he was not the leader of a school. Vanguardist poetry had made itself felt, and the influence of Tablada was more to the point than the spiritual influence of González Martínez. Still the knowledge of his persistent search, of his respect for the European tradition, of his love for French poetry, was a considerable support to the poets associated with the review *Contemporáneos*, whose effort was directed toward understanding and expressing their Mexican reality within the framework of the larger tradition. The only one of these younger poets who shows clearly the influence of EGM is Jaime Torres Bodet, who inherited the deep understanding of Symbolist correspondence.

The last period of EGM's poetry is a renewal of the search for reunion, now expressed in terms of the lost beloved. It was during this period that the poet discovered fully the meaning of his vacillation between heights and abyss, and the occasional joining of the two. And on the basis of this discovery, his poetry projects us onto the bridge that extends into intuited reality, where the aspects of time become one, where all places are the same, where all created things are joined. What González Martínez says to us is surprisingly similar to what we hear from some more recent poets, Octavio Paz among them. And while it is impossible to say what, if any, direct and overt influence there is, the spiritual influence must be admitted.

In recent years the tendency has been to regard Enrique González Martínez more as a monument than as a poet. Everyone grants him a place of honor in Mexican letters—indeed in Hispanic letters generally—but few have read his work except in anthologies. These selections become somewhat standardized and, while they enable us to see some of the moments of beauty, they cannot communicate the poet's discovery of a subtle, intuited reality, or his rebellious dissatisfaction with the limitations characteristic of the human estate. Still the body of poetry was appreciated by those who followed its trajectory, and its influence is part of the poetic tradition, felt and carried on even without reference to the poet's name. It is doubtful that any other poet of his time spoke as directly to what we consider to be the contemporary human dilemma—the consternation of man confronted by the question of what he really is. With González Martínez we move between heights and abyss, experiencing the eternal truth that is contained in the constant presence of choice, and knowing that if the secret is discovered, the vitality of the search will be lost.

Notes and References

Chapter One

1. Napoleon III was interested in spreading his influence to the western hemisphere. He supplied the military strength and encouraged a group of Mexican conservatives to invite the Archduke Maximilian of Austria to become emperor of Mexico. In different circumstances, Maximilian might have been a successful, liberal monarch. But Mexico was a republic. The French intervention interrupted the progress of the Reform Movement, under Benito Juárez, which proposed to establish an orderly progress in the nation by developing it along capitalistic, democratic lines. The liberals fought against the intervention and Napoleon, faced with disapproval of his action at home and abroad, withdrew the French troops. Carlotta, the wife of Maximilian, went to Europe to seek aid. Maximilian was captured and shot on June 19, 1867. The republic was restored.

2. Enrique González Martínez, *Poesía*, 1898-1938. Vol. I. (Mexico: "Polis," 1939), p. 2. Further citations from this collection of three volumes will be identified within parentheses following the quotation, e.g., (I. 162). Other volumes of poetry will be identified by reference to the title of each volume.

3. Frank Dauster, *Breve historia de la poesía mexicana* (Mexico: De Andrea, 1956), p. 121.

4. Enrique González Martínez, *Algunos aspectos de la lírica mexicana* (Mexico: Cultura, 1932).

5. *Ibid.*, pp. 18-19

6. *Ibid.*, p. 28

7. Almost all the biographical information contained in this study is taken from EGM's two volumes of autobiography (see Bibliography). A few additional facts have been taken from the "Cronología" of *La obra de E. G. M.*, the collection of studies published in his honor on his eightieth birthday (see Bibliography).

8. *Preludios, Lirismos, Silénter, Los Senderos Ocultos* (Mexico: Porrúa, 1946), p. 24. The "Polis" collection does not contain all the poems from the first two volumes. It begins with *La hora inútil* which contains a selection from the two.

9. Enrique González Martínez, *Cuentos y otras páginas*. Prólogo y selección de Ana María Sánchez (Mexico: Libro-Mex, 1955).

10. In his "Prólogo" to the *Preludios*, etc. published by Porrúa, pp. vii-ix.

11. The word *fuente* offers great difficulty in dealing with EGM's poetry for an English-reading audience. The word can mean "fountain," but it has a strong sense of "source." EGM means the stream of fresh water that one finds in nature. Unfortunately, the English word "spring" has a variety of meanings that can be confusing, but it does have the feeling of "source" that *fuente* has.

Chapter Two

1. "Psalle et sile" is perhaps best translated as "Sing Quietly." Since EGM used the Latin phrase as the title of his poem, it is more in keeping with the spirit of his work to retain the title untranslated. He uses Latin and French titles rather frequently. In general, the meanings are more readily apparent than in this poem.

2. *Literatura española*, siglo XX, 2nd edition (Mexico: Antigua Librería Robredo, 1949), pp. 45-66. The essay is also included in *La obra de E. G. M.* (Colegio Nacional, Mexico, 1951), pp. 231-36.

3. *A través de libros y de autores* (Buenos Aires: Nuestra América, 1925), pp. 217-42. Also in *La obra de E. G. M.*, pp. 86-100. The specific reference is to p. 93.

Chapter Three

1. Dauster, p. 121.

2. The word "vanguardist," as I use it here, is simply another way of saying "avant-garde." It is a convenient way of referring to the various groups, movements, and manifestos that had many different names and particular characteristics, but shared the revolutionary intent of finding a radically new expression.

3. The device in this poem is slightly more complicated than usual. A separated couplet follows the third stanza. Then another couplet is syntactically joined to the following quatrain. This technical procedure establishes the transition satisfactorily, and its peculiarity seems to be of no significance to the meaning of the poem.

4. I am indebted to Gary Brower for his detailed study of the influence of *haiku* in Spanish America, unpublished at this writing.

Chapter Four

1. An abridgement of this address may be found in the Sánchez edition of EGM's *Cuentos y otras páginas,* pp. 107-26.

2. The literary scene in Mexico was very interesting and very complicated. The major effort in poetry was the review, *Contemporáneos,* whose collaborators included some of the best poets Mexico has produced: Torres Bodet, Villaurrutia, Pellicer, Nandino, Novo,

Cuesta, Ortiz de Montellano, Owen, and others including EGM's son, Enrique González Rojo. The literary world, seeking the expression of the new Mexico, was embroiled in a debate between nativists and universalists.

3. The dates of composition of the individual poems are not given in this volume. EGM's son, Enrique González Rojo, was a well-established poet by the time *Unfinished Poems* was published. However, the poems contained in it obviously cover a considerable span of time. The first volume of the son's poems was published in 1924.

4. Two others that combine well with "Nakedness" are "Transparency" ("Diafanidad") and "Clarity" ("Claridad").

5. The poem is printed on a prefatory, unnumbered page of the third volume of *Poesía, 1898-1938* (Mexico: Polis, 1939-1940).

6. The title of the poem is in English.

7. *Op. cit.*, p. 93.

8. The part of the volume that properly belongs to the title is only thirty-five pages long. However, it also contains *The Flood of Fire, Babel* (both published in earlier volumes), and *Beginning and End of the Sea*, another long poem which the editors of this volume properly include with the two poems mentioned above.

Chapter Five

1. I have used the "Polis" edition of the *Poesías* because it is easy to handle. *The Flood of Fire* is also in *The New Narcissus*.

2. This essay was expanded in *Indology* (*Indología*). If we were to pursue this line of understanding EGM, his insistence on sensitivity might also cause us to relate his work to the spiritual qualities of the Latin American which are emphasized in José Enrique Rodó's *Ariel* (1900).

3. This edition was published by the *Revista de Literatura Mexicana*. Its format is beautiful and the printing is superb, but the pages are not numbered. Therefore, I will use the edition that appeared as part of *The New Narcissus*, and page references will be to that volume.

Selected Bibliography

PRIMARY SOURCES

1. Poetry

Poesía, 1898-1938 (Mexico: "Polis," Vols. I & II, 1939, Vol. III, 1940). This collection opens with *La hora inútil,* which is a selection from EGM's first two books, *Preludios* and *Lirismos.* From that point forward, it includes all the poetry through *Tres rosas en el ánfora,* and ends with the volume of translations from French, *Los jardines de Francia.*

Preludios, Lirismos, Silénter, Los senderos ocultos, ed. Antonio Castro Leal (Mexico: Porrúa, 1946). Contains the first four volumes of EGM's poetry complete.

Bajo el signo mortal (Mexico: Poesía Hispanoamericana, 1942).

Segundo despertar y otros poemas (Mexico: Stylo, 1945).

Vilano al viento (Mexico: Stylo, 1948).

Babel (Mexico: Revista de literatura Mexicana, 1949).

El nuevo Narciso y otros poemas (Mexico: Fondo de Cultura Económica, 1952).

2. Translations of Poetry into English

BLACKWELL, ALICE STONE. *Some Spanish American Poets,* 2nd ed. (Philadelphia: University of Pennsylvania, 1937).

CRAIG, G. DUNDAS. *The Modernist Trend in Spanish American Poetry* (Berkeley: University of California, 1934).

JOHNSON, MILDRED E. *Swan, Cygnets, and Owl* (Columbia: University of Missouri Studies, 1956). Contains "Tuércele el cuello al cisne," "¿Te acuerdas?", "Cuando sepas hallar una sonrisa," "Como hermana y hermano," "El retorno imposible."

JONES, WILLIS KNAPP, ed. *Spanish American Literature in Translation: A Selection of Poetry, Fiction and Drama Since 1888* (New York: Frederick Ungar, 1963). Contains "Tuércele el cuello al cisne," "La plegaria de la roca estéril," "Mañana los poetas."

PANE, REMIGIO UGO. "Three Mexican Poets: Sor Juana Inés de la Cruz, Manuel Gutiérrez Nájera, and Enrique González Martínez. A Bibliography of Their Poems in English Translation," *Bulletin of Bibliography,* 18, 10 (May-Aug. 1946), 233-34. Lists poems contained in books cited here which were published prior to 1946, also many in periodicals.

PAZ, OCTAVIO, compiler and BECKETT, SAMUEL, trans. *Anthology of Mexican Poetry* (Bloomington: Indiana University, 1958). Contains "Tuércele el cuello al cisne," "Cuando sepas hallar una sonrisa," "Casa con dos puertas," "Dolor," "Romance del muerto vivo," "Ultimo viaje."

UNDERWOOD, E. W. *Anthology of Mexican Poets* (Portland, Maine: Mosher, 1932).

3. Prose

Algunos aspectos de la lírica mexicana (Mexico: Cultura, 1932).
El hombre del buho (Mexico: Cuadernos Americanos, 1944).
La apacible locura (Mexico: Cuadernos Americanos, 1951).
Cuentos y otras páginas, ed. Ana María Sánchez (Mexico: Libro-Mex, 1955).

SECONDARY SOURCES

La obra de Enrique González Martínez, ed. José Luis Martínez (Mexico: Colegio Nacional, 1951). Contains chronology, bibliography of EGM's work, and sixty-two critical articles and tributes to the poet. Basic for study of EGM. Many of the best studies are included. Some of the most helpful of these will be listed separately below, showing original place of publication and location in this volume.

AVRETT, ROBERT. "Enrique González Martínez, Philosopher and Mystic," *Hispania,* XIV, 3 (May, 1931) 183-92. Observations on EGM's poetic quest through *Las señales furtivas.* Attempts to reconcile "mysticism" and "philosophy."

BENGE, FRANCES. *La biografía lírica de Enrique González Martínez* (Mexico: Universidad Autónoma de México, 1924). An essay of thirty pages, interesting mainly for author's view of the poet in 1924. Considers his latest book, *El romero alucinado,* his greatest achievement, and discusses its vanguardist aspects.

CASTRO LEAL, ANTONIO. "Prólogo" to *Preludios,* etc. (Mexico: Porrúa, 1946), pp. vii-xiii. Also in *La obra de E. G. M.,* pp. 210-13. Relationship of EGM's poetry to Parnassian and Symbolist poetry; the basic influence of Horace; influence of Pagaza and Díaz Mirón; growth of EGM's poetic independence.

COLIN, EDUARDO. "Enrique González Martínez," in *Verbo selecto* (Mexico: México Moderno, 1922), pp. 51-56. Also in *La obra de E. G. M.,* pp. 78-85. Relationship of idea and emotion in EGM's poetry.

DAUSTER, FRANK. *Breve historia de la poesía mexicana* (Mexico: De Andrea, 1956). Pages 118-21 are a brief but careful and accurate statement of the trajectory of EGMs' poetry, describing the major changes.

ENGLEKIRK, JOHN E. et al. *An Outline History of Spanish American Literature* (New York: Appleton-Century-Crofts, 1965). Pages 129-31 contain brief, very general description of work, suggested reading, texts, editions, translations, critical references.

FERNANDEZ MACGREGOR, GENARO. "El poeta en el tumulto," *El Universal*, (March 25, 1949), pp. 3, 13. Also in *La obra de E. G. M.*, pp. 240-44. With particular reference to *Babel*, discusses the combination of muse and beloved in EGM's poetry.

GOLDBERG, ISAAC. *Studies in Spanish American Literature* (New York: Brentano's, 1920). Discussion of general characteristics, pp. 82-92, with emphasis on "pantheism." Some translations by Blackwell.

HENRIQUEZ URENA, PEDRO. "Prólogo" to *Jardines de Francia* (Mexico: Porrúa, 1915), pp. ix-xxi. Examines poetry of EGM in the perspective of literary movements.

LEIVA, RAUL. *Imagen de la poesía mexicana contemporánea* (Mexico: Imprenta Universitaria, 1959). Pages 23-32 are a general discussion, main interest is in swan controversy. Reads suggestion of Anglo imperialism in EGM's socially committed poems.

LUISI, LUISA. "La poesía de Enrique González Martínez," in *A través de libros y de autores* (Buenos Aires: "Nuestra América," 1925), pp. 217-42. Also in *La obra de E. G. M.*, pp. 88-100. EGM and other poets of the time; EGM's refusal of the easy answer; sees irony of *El romero alucinado* as a phase in the poet's career.

PAZ, OCTAVIO. "Introduction to the History of Mexican Poetry," in *An Anthology of Mexican Poetry* (Bloomington: Indiana University, 1958). EGM's relationship with *modernismo*, believes EGM was "the first to give poetry a sense of the gravity of words."

REYES NEVARES, SALVADOR. "La literatura mexicana en el siglo XX-I (1900-1930)," in *Panorama das literaturas das Américas*, Vol. IV, (Angola: Edição do Municipio de Nova Lisboa), pp. 1980-84. One of the clearest short descriptions of EGM's poetry. Describes difference between poet's admonition and spiritual adventure, sense of passage through life, EGM's tendency to discover things rather than classify them.

SALINAS, PEDRO. "El cisne y el buho," in *Literatura española*, 2nd ed. (Mexico: Antigua Librería de Robredo, 1949), pp. 45-65. Also in *La obra de E. G. M.*, pp. 147-65. The best and most complete study of EGM and *modernismo*.

SANCHEZ, ANA MARIA. "Bibliografías mexicanas contemporáneas V: Enrique González Martínez (1871-1952)," *Boletín de la Biblioteca Nacional*, segunda epoca, VIII, 2 (April-June, 1957), 16-72. Exhaustive bibliography of EGM's work, criticism of his work, and testimonials to the man and his work. More than 450 entries.

————. "Prólogo" to *Cuentos y otras páginas*, pp. 7-18. The only discussion of EGM's prose.

TOPETE, JOSE MANUEL. "González Martínez y la crítica," *Revista Iberoamericana*, XVI, 32 (Jan., 1951), 255-66. Excellent account of criticism on EGM, showing what aspects of his work are emphasized by what critics, and what opinions have become standard.

————. "La muerte del cisne (?)," *Hispania*, XXXVI, 3 (Aug., 1953), 273-77. Agrees with Salinas regarding EGM and *modernismo*; shows persistence of swan image in EGM's poetry.

————. "El ritmo poético de Enrique González Martínez," *Revista Iberoamericana*, XVIII, 35 (Dec., 1952), 131-39. Quantitative analysis of versification, related to themes and periods of EGM's work.

TOUSSAINT, MANUEL. "Prólogo" to *Los cien mejores poemas de Enrique González Martínez* (Mexico: Cultura, 1920), pp. 7-32. Also in *La obra de E. G. M.*, pp. 60-77. Very thoughtful study of development of EGM's poetry through *Parábolas* and into *La palabra del viento* (then unpublished). Particular attention to influences, and to the blending of one volume into the next.

Index